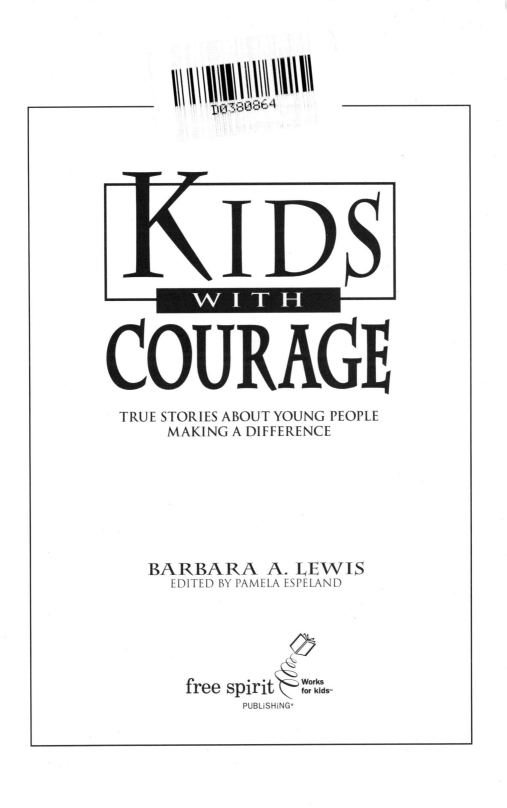

# KIDS WITH COURAGE

## TRUE STORIES ABOUT YOUNG PEOPLE MAKING A DIFFERENCE

### BARBARA A. LEWIS
EDITED BY PAMELA ESPELAND

free spirit

Works
for kids™

PUBLiSHiNG®

D0380864

**Library of Congress Cataloging-in-Publication Data**
Lewis, Barbara A., 1943–
　　Kids with courage : true stories about young people making a difference / by Barbara A. Lewis ; edited by Pamela Espeland.
　　　　p.　　cm.
　　Includes index.
　　Summary: Relates the stories of kids who made a difference in their neighborhood, community, or the world by helping in such areas as crime, life-saving, and the environment.
　　ISBN 0-915793-39-3
　　1. United States—Biography—Juvenile literature. 2. Heroes—United States—Biography—Juvenile literature. 3. Children—United States—Biography—Juvenile literature. 4. Life-saving—United States—Juvenile literature. 5. Courage—Juvenile literature.
　　[1. Heroes.] I. Espeland, Pamela, 1951–　　. II. Title.
CT217.L497　　1992
920'.0083—dc20
　　[B]　　　　　　　　　　　　　　　　　　　　　　　　　　　91-46726
　　　　　　　　　　　　　　　　　　　　　　　　　　　　　　　　CIP
　　　　　　　　　　　　　　　　　　　　　　　　　　　　　　　　AC

Cover and book design by MacLean & Tuminelly

10　9　8　7
Printed in the United States of America

**Free Spirit Publishing Inc.**
400 First Avenue North, Suite 616
Minneapolis, MN 55401
(612) 338-2068

# DEDICATION

To Andrea, who's always had the courage
to do hard things.

This book is also dedicated to you young people
who so generously shared your stories,
each tossing one stone into the water.
May your single acts become many.
May your courageous actions ripple out to sea.

# ACKNOWLEDGMENTS

Thanks to my publisher, Judy Galbraith, who believes that kids can accomplish miracles. And to my editor, Pamela Espeland, who actually accomplishes miracles.

A special tribute to the young people in this book and all their parents, teachers, and officials who helped make their projects more successful.

I would like to express gratitude to the following organizations, which shared information and expertise in the preparation of this book: Future Problem Solving Program, National Crime Prevention Council, U.S. Department of Justice, United Nations Youth Environment Programme, U.S. Environmental Protection Agency Youth Program, Hitachi Foundation, Parker Vogelsinger & Associates, The Giraffe Project, Sea Breeze—Clairol Corporation, National Safety Council, U.S. Consumer Product Safety Commission, Utah Natural Resources, Utah Highway Safety, National Rifle Association, Utah Emergency Medical Training Council, National Highway Traffic Safety Administration, American Academy of Pediatrics.

An extra acknowledgment to my husband, Larry, and my children, Mike, Andrea, Christian, and Samuel, for their patience and encouragement.

And lastly, thanks to my cleaning ladies, Jetta and Debbie, without whose assistance this book probably would not have been completed.

# CONTENTS

Introduction      1

## KIDS FIGHTING CRIME      5

### A Serious Habit      11
*Charles Carson was a runaway and a drug addict.  Now he counsels kids and battles violence, drugs, and crime.*

### Fear and Flashbacks      19
*Mr. Smith threatened to kill her mother and brother. But Mercedes Jones spoke out anyway—and a sexual abuser went to jail.*

### "That's My Big Sister!"      27
*Keema McAdoo's after-school programs keep kids off the streets and away from drugs.*

### Crime Watching Pays at Southridge High      33
*When a student got shot after a basketball game, the Spartan Patrol flew into action.*

## Dreams, Threats, and Sweaty Palms     41

*Norvell Smith knew there would be gang members in
the audience. But she looked right at them and gave
them a piece of her mind.*

# KIDS TAKING
# SOCIAL ACTION     49

## Honoring Their Ancestors     55

*To Rena and Jenna Duncan, those statues in the
Capitol Building weren't just two anonymous Indians.
They were John Duncan and Unca Som.*

## Fighting for Kids' Rights     65

*Joby Shimomura knew that kids had something to
say...if adults would only listen.*

## Hearing Disabled,
## Not Mentally Disabled     73

*For years, people have tried to tell Samuel Long,
"You can't do that." But Sam never hears them.*

## Reaching Out to a Stranger     81

*It was the middle of winter, and the woman had no
shoes. Frank Daily looked down at his Nikes and
made a decision.*

# HEROIC KIDS

## Gun Control 91
*The student had a loaded gun and a room full of hostages. Police surrounded the school. Then Ruben Ortega got mad.*

## Saving a Busload of Children 99
*Something was wrong with the driver, and the bus was rushing toward trees. Could Carl Boney and Michael Etowski move fast enough?*

## Courage in a Fire 105
*The house was filled with smoke and flames. And Melinda Clark couldn't find her little brother.*

## Rescuing a Friend from Drowning 111
*The boys fell into the icy water. Heavy, wet winter coats dragged them down. Then Andy D'Alesio saved the life of his friend.*

## Five Days in a Mine 117
*His dad thought he was with the older boys. They thought he was with his dad. But Joshua Dennis was alone in the dark, deep underground, with nothing but his faith.*

# KIDS SAVING THE ENVIRONMENT

129

## Starting a Club to Save the Elephants    135

*Elephants are big. Second-graders are small. But that didn't stop the Fowlers.*

## Saving the Wetlands    143

*Andrew Holleman had practically grown up on the wetlands. He loved its plants, creatures, and gooey mud. Then he heard about the developer's plan.*

## Testing the Waters    151

*Beans wouldn't grow in it. Pond snails died in it. There was something wrong with the water in the T.J. drain, and Kevin Bell had the proof in his notebook.*

## "Kids for Saving Earth"    157

*Thousands of kids around the world keep Clinton Hill's dream alive.*

## Index    165
## About the Author    175

# INTRODUCTION

## WHY READ TRUE STORIES ABOUT REAL KIDS?

Have you ever looked into a mirror, or seen yourself reflected in a pond or a lake? That image is not really you, but you can learn a lot about yourself by studying it. You can tell if you're healthy and fit, if you've been eating and sleeping enough. You can see your mood and your personality. Do you have frown wrinkles or laugh lines? Do you look worried or peaceful?

The stories in this book are like your reflection. They aren't really about you, but they are about other kids like you, and you can learn a lot about yourself by reading them. Do you wish you could do courageous things? Would you like to make a difference in your neighborhood, your community, your world? You can see that it's possible, once you meet other kids who show you the way.

These young people are not famous Americans who lived long ago. They're kids of the 90's. They're battling the same problems you are. Because they aren't famous, rich, or powerful, you can believe that *anyone* can do courageous and wonderful things. Even you.

If you drop a stone into a pond over your reflection, your face ripples out of focus. Your image disappears and then wobbles before you. But it all slides back into place, and there you are again. Reading these stories is like dropping a stone into water. For a moment, you forget about yourself. As you study these reflections of other kids' lives, you share their thoughts and their struggles, maybe giggle or cry with them. Then, when you're through reading, you slide back into yourself again. Still you—except you're stronger somehow, or smarter, or braver. You have grown.

# HOW TO READ THIS BOOK

You can munch right in and devour the whole book. Or you can open the table of contents and nibble only those stories that interest you.

Would you like to meet someone who has tackled a problem similar to one you are facing—pollution, kids' rights, crime, how to cope with an emergency? If you look carefully, you might find someone who can inspire you to solve your problem.

You'll see that this book has four main sections: Kids Fighting Crime, Kids Taking Social Action, Heroic Kids, and Kids Saving the Environment. Each section begins with a short introduction to get you started thinking about the issues and relating them to your own life. There are tips you can follow to learn and do more. How far you go is up to you.

# WHAT TO DO WHEN YOU'RE THROUGH READING

Do you have problems similar to those the young people in this book experienced? Do these kids make you want to do something to improve your world?

You can see from their examples how they began their projects. You may want to follow a similar path. Or you might choose to ask a trusted adult to help you start working on solutions. You may want to invite other kids to join your team.

The real purpose of this book is to help you know that *you can control things that happen around you and to you.* Sometimes this takes a serious commitment and great effort. And sometimes it's as simple as speaking out on how you feel.

What's important to know is that the future belongs to you. You're the one who must decide the course of your life. You can choose to change your world for the better.

# WHAT'S YOUR STORY?

Through the stories in this book, you will discover that anyone, at any age, in any life circumstance, can make a difference. You'll meet Ruben Ortega, who disarmed a young man shooting a rifle at a high school. And Norvell Smith, who conquered her own fears and spoke out against gangs. And Joshua Dennis, who survived five days alone in a mine without food or water. And other kids who fought back, came to the rescue, and stood up for what they believed in. These are all true stories about real kids. With one exception, you'll even learn their real names.

How did these kids get to be so courageous? Read their stories, think about them, talk them over with your friends, parents, and teachers, then decide for yourself what makes these young people special. Afterward, take a look at your own life. Imagine that you are writing *your* story. In what ways have you been courageous or special? Write down your story and send it to me. There may be another *Kids with Courage* book someday. And you may be part of it.

Here is where to send your story:

> Barbara A. Lewis
> c/o Free Spirit Publishing Inc.
> 400 First Avenue North, Suite 616
> Minneapolis, MN 55401

I'd like to hear from you.

> Barbara Lewis
> January 1992

# KIDS
# FIGHTING
# CRIME

*W*hich of these is most likely to become a crime victim?

    *a. an elderly person*

    *b. a middle-aged person*

    *c. a teenager*

    *d. a child*

*If you answered "c," you're right. More crimes are committed against young people ages 12 to 19 than any other age group in the United States. Every 19 seconds, a teenager is the target of a crime.*

*Almost 70 percent of these crimes involve property theft, but teens are also victims of assault, rape, murder, and everything else. If you were to fill a school with 2,000 teens, about 360 of them would have been victims of crime in the past year. \**

*What can you do about crime? "Nothing," you might think, "because I'm only one person." But that isn't true. You are about to read real stories about real kids who are fighting crime, individually and in groups. These kids are making a difference.*

*You'll meet Charles Carson, a teenage "nobody" who lived in the streets, then transformed himself into a crime-fighting, drug-battling somebody. And "Mercedes," a teenager who was sexually abused as a child, but had the courage to tell her story and now helps other victims. And Keema McAdoo, who puts in many volunteer hours teaching younger children about the dangers of drugs. And Southridge High students Sandy St. Amand and Barbara Castro, leaders in a group that has solved several school and neighborhood*

---

\* Statistics are from the National Crime Prevention Council, 1700 K. Street, N.W., Second Floor, Washington, D.C. 20006; (202) 466-6272.

*crimes. And Norvell Smith, a young Chicago girl who stood up and spoke out against gang violence.*

*There may have been a time when each of these kids thought, "I can't do anything about crime." They don't think that way anymore.*

## DON'T BE A VICTIM: 12 TIPS FOR AVOIDING CRIME

Each year, millions of young people become crime victims. How can you protect yourself? Follow these tips to lower your risk.

**1.** Use the buddy system. Don't go places alone, especially at night. Stay away from poorly lighted, secluded spots.

**2.** Always let a trustworthy person know where you are and when you will be coming home. Tell a parent, a grandparent, an older sister or brother, a close friend, or a neighbor you can count on.

**3.** Trust your instincts. If a situation doesn't feel right to you, get away and get help.

**4.** Always keep a quarter in your pocket for an emergency phone call.

**5.** Keep valuables out of sight. Lock them in the trunk of your car, keep them in your (locked) locker at school, or leave them at home.

**6.** Don't hitchhike or go home from parties with strangers or new acquaintances.

**7.** Don't get involved with drugs or alcohol.

**8.** Wear clothing and shoes that give you the freedom to run.

**9.** Lock your doors and windows, even during the day. And don't open your door to strangers. If you are traveling in a car, lock that door, too.

**10.** Don't give out personal information (your name, address, etc.) on the phone. And never tell anyone that you are home alone.

**11.** Don't give anyone your house keys or let anyone copy them, not even your friends.

**12.** Report any crimes or suspected crimes at once. If you are a victim, the best thing you can do is to report it right away. Tell an adult who can help you. Call the police or go to the police.

# A SERIOUS HABIT

*Charles Carson was a runaway and a drug addict. Now he counsels kids and battles violence, drugs, and crime.*

There's a billboard in Tacoma, Washington that reads: "Guns and knives are taking lives—Who's next?" And another: "You can't stop THE violence...But you can stop YOUR violence."

You might guess that some big advertising agency had invented these clever slogans. But you would be wrong. They were created by a 19-year-old with a dream, a guy who cares so much about kids that he has spent thousands of hours at the local Boys Club inspiring, coaching, and instructing young people.

What motivated Charles Carson to wage his own war against drugs, crime, and violence? What got him on local TV, radio, and the CBS National News with Dan Rather? He must be famous; he must have gone to all the right schools; he must have a dad who's at least a district attorney...right?

Wrong again. His father deserted the family when Charles was seven, leaving Charles's mom, Linda, to raise four kids including Charles, his older brother Tony, and his younger siblings Jeremy and

Lydia. Charles grew up at home and in a series of foster homes. And for much of his childhood, he lived on the streets, a runaway and a drug addict.

"I didn't feel I belonged," he says. "I started using drugs when I was nine years old. By ten, I was addicted to marijuana. At sixteen, I was using cocaine and had developed a serious habit."

To support his drug habit, Charles started stealing. He was arrested and sent to detention homes 18 times for crimes including burglary, arson, even forgery. "All these offenses were drug-related," he explains.

Charles remembers sitting on his bed in his basement bedroom when he was 15. He knew things weren't right in his life. His room was plastered with posters of his hero, Prince, a rock star. And Charles began thinking, "I wonder how Prince became such a success? He had a tough beginning....

"I knew my friends had moms and dads. All the basic family stuff. I knew it wasn't there for me. I had to accept that. I argued with my younger brother and sister. I didn't help them. I knew this was wrong. I thought there was something strange about our family. I had no one to talk to who could feel the way I felt. I didn't want anyone to tell me things were okay, when I knew they weren't. I cried a lot."

After living in several foster homes, Charles dropped out of school in the tenth grade and ran away. He managed to stay alive by stealing food from stores and people's homes. He slept under houses and in garages; sometimes he just walked through the night. He remembers one time when he and his brother stayed in a house with no heat. "It was in the winter. It was cold. We turned the oven on and sat in chairs in front of the oven and finally slept."

Charles tells that while he lived on the streets, "I dealt drugs to get drugs....I saw everything—killings, overdoses, even among my relatives.

"People have prejudices and stereotypes about street life. They don't really know what's going on. Street knowledge should be a class. Like, one time I was standing with this guy in the streets. Some Cubans came up to him to do a drug deal. They started arguing in Spanish. One of the Cubans pulled out a .22 automatic and shot the guy in the chest. He blasted him on the left side, right below his ribs. Then they ran off.

"Everybody left him right there. It was a bad drug area. It shocked me that people didn't care. Someone's life was less important than the drug deal. I waited for the police and told the story."

Charles began to change, but it didn't happen overnight. And it wasn't easy. "When you tamper with drugs," he says, "there are only two ways to go. One is down hill, and the other is dead, and you don't get to choose which one.

"But one day I was walking along. I saw other human beings staggering down the street talking to the wind, not knowing who they were, their brains all whacked out on drugs. They'd be walking around for the rest of their lives. No job. Nothing.

"I knew I had no home, no friends, only the ragged clothes on my back. I walked for a long time. The weather was gray and dreary, the kind of day that would seem depressing even if everything was right. It finally dawned on me that there was only me and God. I always believed in God.

"I thought of my mom. I remembered the first time I was arrested in sixth grade and how she came and tried to get me out. She brought me beef jerky to show she loved me. She knew I liked it and wouldn't forget that. My mom taught me everything I knew—to cook, iron, sew, every basic thing. Like, I'd ask her how to iron and she'd get on my case until I got it right. I learned to be a great ironer when I was ten. She preached to me. I guess my mom knew I was going to be an 'on-your-own' person.

"I decided to call my mom. I went to a phone. She talked to me. She said, 'You control your actions. People give you good and bad advice. Evaluate it. Turn it to work best for you. You have to blame yourself for decisions.'

"I put the phone down and kept on walking. I began to develop a personal hunger. I wanted to be something great. Not great in the sense of fame, but great in the sense of care and love. This was my real turning point.

"I still screwed up, but I started to do opposite things. Like, I'd skip a drug deal or only do one to get food. I would take more control of my actions and the consequences. What I *had* been doing was telling lies and tricking myself....

"I talked to God. I would say, 'Would Jesus want me to do this?' I developed a faith in God, knowing that He is real.

"I started going to the Boys Club. I played basketball, started lifting weights, and began playing the guitar. I found the choices I was making were right. I started using drugs less. On June 2, 1988, I went cold turkey. I just stopped using."

Charles cared about other kids and wanted to help them, to keep them from making the same mistakes he had made. He was hired as the Boys and Girls Clubs' first minority staff volunteer. He began talking with kids and became a role model not only for younger kids, but also for his peers and his family.

He designed his own self-esteem class at the Boys Club, where he counseled kids and his peers on a one-to-one basis. "There are a lot of me's out there," he says. "The way to stop drugs is to stop them in individual lives. Then there would be no demand for drugs. What will make you quit drugs is finding out who you are within yourself."

Charles's program expanded to include over 50 kids at the Boys Club. "The little kids started calling me

'Daddy,'" he says proudly. "It's a great feeling." He trudged the streets and pulled in dropouts and wandering kids. At the Boys Club, he taught them weight lifting and basketball. He encouraged junior-high youth to write plays about making good choices, which they performed for elementary schools.

Kids listened to him—kids like Darren, a ten-year-old tyrant. Darren was skinny, curly-haired, and wanted to join a gang. "He was smart enough to know his world wasn't right," Charles relates. "He told me, 'Why should I even try to be good? My mom isn't anything. She uses drugs. She tells me not to. But she uses them.'

"I told him he doesn't have to live the way someone else does. I took him to play basketball and to movies. I even took him with me when I went shopping. I wanted him to see that I was able to do the same things everyone

**Charles Carson, center, coaches basketball at the Eastside Boys and Girls Club in Tacoma, Washington.** Photo by Bruce Kellman/Tacoma Morning News Tribune. January 1990.

else can do.  It's not the end of the road when you have big problems.

"Darren's doing good today.  He has a little trouble in school.  But he listens to me.  He's not on drugs.  And he's not in a gang."

During this time, Charles went back to high school and completed four years of requirements in two years of work.  He was 19 when he graduated.  Soon after, he was selected to attend the Washington Governor's School for Citizen Leadership at Seattle University.

Today Charles works for the Tacoma Youth Initiative. His job is to recruit troubled youth for community service.  He has also spoken out against drugs on radio and

**Charles Carson distributes posters for the Tacoma Youth Initiative sponsored by Safe Streets to Tacoma area businesses.** Photo by Karen Stallwood/Tacoma Morning News Tribune.

television. Plus he has designed and put his anti-drug, anti-violence messages on billboards around the city.

Meanwhile, Charles is attending Tacoma Community College. Soon he will transfer to the University of Puget Sound, where he will work toward a degree in sociology and human services.

"My dream is to marry my girlfriend," Charles says. "Also, I'd like to see the races come together. We could have so much more. There have been so many quarrels. And I'd like to see honesty everywhere, and unity. And I wish I was a billionaire, because then I could do something. I could invest my money in kids, send them to college, get them off the streets, if I had the money."

# FEAR AND FLASHBACKS

*Mr. Smith threatened to kill her mother and brother. But Mercedes Jones spoke out anyway—and a sexual abuser went to jail.*

Mercedes Jones* is 16 years old now. She lives in Louisville, Kentucky. She's on her high-school swimming team, has won zillions of ribbons for gymnastics, and has served in student government. She's well-liked, bubbly, and very brave.

It's been nine years since her nightmare ended, but Mercedes still has flashbacks which sometimes awaken her at night with a jolt and a scream. Jane, her mother, comes into her room and pulls her daughter close, brushing back the tangle of damp hair, while Mercedes quivers in her mother's arms like a frightened puppy. Her mom invites her to talk until her shaking ends. The drops of sweat dry on Mercedes' forehead, leaving cool tracks behind.

Mercedes was only three years old when she first entered the Smith home to be babysat. Her mother, recently divorced, had to go to work to support Mercedes and her older brother. The home

---

* "Mercedes Jones" is not the real name of the young woman in this story. All of the names in this story have been changed.

day-care center Jane had chosen for her daughter looked great. Mrs. Smith, who ran the place and kept it spotless, seemed like a very nice woman. Mr. Smith was friendly and kind. The couple had two children of their own and babysat an additional six or seven children.

At first Mercedes didn't understand what was happening to her. But for the next four years during nap time, she was sexually abused by Mr. Smith. When she struggled, Mr. Smith flashed knives in her face or held a gun to her temple, telling her he would kill her mother and brother if she told anyone. Mercedes learned later that Mrs. Smith had known what her husband was doing; she just never tried to stop him.

Mercedes has blocked many of the memories from her mind, partly in self-defense. She is a survivor. "It's strange, but he never told me he'd kill me," she recalls. "He always said he'd kill my mother and brother."

When Mercedes was eight, a year after she had stopped staying at the Smith house, her mother read a newspaper article about a child who had been sexually abused. She spoke frankly to her children, as she always did, warning them that if anyone ever tried to hurt them in this way, they should tell her about it, even if they were threatened.

The dam broke. Mercedes let loose and poured out years of fears and buried emotions. She clung to her mother and felt Jane's body stiffen in anger as Mercedes added details. Her mom's face reddened. They cried together.

"You are very brave," her mom told her. "What happened to you is not your fault. It's no different than if someone gets robbed or beaten up on the streets, or if someone steals your wallet. These are all crimes. And the victim of a crime is *never, ever* guilty."

Mercedes and her mother went to the police the next morning and reported the abuse. "There was one policeman there, Sergeant Wally," Mercedes remembers. "He was really nice to me. He made me laugh. He was really cool." She would see him many more times after that.

As a result of Mercedes' testimony, Mr. Smith was arrested and jailed. But that wasn't the end of it for Mercedes. "When I was eight, my friends didn't understand," she explains, lowering her head. "They'd say things like, 'She's so freaky. So weird.'"

Mercedes transferred from a public school to a private school, where her mother worked as a secretary. "I changed so I could be near her, because it was so hard to go on with a normal life," Mercedes says. "She was always there. She was everything to me. At nights, when I had nightmares, she'd let me sleep with her, even though I kicked hard all the time."

Shortly after Mr. Smith was arrested, Mercedes was riding in the car with her mom. All of a sudden, "my mom freaked out. There was this guy jogging at the side of the road. It was him! I was scared to death all over. My mom was so shaken she almost ran into him with the car. It took all her self-control to keep from running over him. She pulled the car over and stopped."

They later learned that Mr. Smith was out on bail, awaiting trial. Mercedes knew that she would have to testify against him at the trial. She was already worried about that. Now he was on the streets again. What if he followed through on his threats? What if he tried to kill her mom and her brother?

Once Jane asked Mercedes if there was anything she could have told her to prevent what had happened. Mercedes looked up at her with wide, blue eyes. She fiddled with the sleeve of her oversized flannel shirt. "Mom, you never told me he wouldn't really kill anybody—that I didn't need to believe him." Jane pulled Mercedes close.

The trial was delayed several times. Mercedes was anxious to put the ordeal behind her. A full year and a half after the arrest, Mercedes testified against Mr. Smith in court. Four little boys came forward to join her in testifying against the molester.

On the day of the trial, Mercedes fidgeted with her hair. She choked down her orange juice, but didn't touch her cereal. She didn't want to see Mr. Smith ever again. They arrived at 8:00 a.m. and were placed in the office opposite the courtroom. People had donated toys to the children, and they tried to play and watch TV. Sergeant Wally arrived to joke with the kids and to try to put them at ease.

"But I was so mad because of what this man was doing to my life," Mercedes says. "Everybody knew. There were TV reporters crawling all over. I was scared people would laugh at me. And I didn't want to cry in front of people. I was a 'tomgirl,' and it's not cool to cry. But I had to go in there and describe every disgusting thing.

"I was so scared! I was really afraid he was going to get me if I testified. But I knew I had to be brave so he wouldn't ever do this to anyone else."

When Mercedes went to be sworn in, she saw Mr. Smith. Suddenly her blood turned to ice. "I didn't look at him after that first glimpse. It was easier not to look at him. I just looked at my mother."

As the children took their turns on the stand, the defense lawyer tried to confuse them. "He tried to make it look like all five of us had gotten together and planned this. One little boy was only four years old!" Mercedes shakes her head. "The lawyer tried to make it look like *we* were guilty, like it was *our* fault.

"The little four-year-old was amazing. He told the defense lawyer, 'My attorney said you'd try to confuse me, and you are confusing me. So stop it.'" The people in the courtroom laughed. The lawyer's face turned red.

Soon it was Mercedes' turn. She sank into the chair cushion and sat on her knees. The arms of the chair reached nearly to her neck.

"The defense lawyer asked me if we kids ever got together other than at the babysitter," she says. "I know now that he was trying to prove we had conspired or made the whole thing up. But I didn't know it then. I just said 'Yeah.' And he wanted to know where we had gotten together. I said, 'At the pool.' He asked what we talked about. I said, 'Who could swim the fastest.'"

The people in the courtroom roared again. The lawyer ran his finger inside his shirt collar.

Throughout the questioning, Mercedes tried very hard to be brave. When her chin quivered, she looked at her mom. She only cried a little bit as her teeth dug into her lips. But when she finished she stepped down, faced the court with her head held high, and smiled. She had told the truth, and she was proud of herself for doing it.

Mr. Smith was convicted of five felonies and misdemeanors for molesting the children. Investigators estimated that he had victimized as many as 40 children. But, they hoped, he would never do it again. Mr. Smith was sentenced to 25 years in prison.

After the trial, Mercedes tried to put it all behind her. She developed new friendships. Most of the time, people treated her with the respect she deserved. Then one boy she shared her story with looked at her and said, "You must have a disease." He called her a slut and walked away.

But Mercedes is a survivor and a fighter. She pursued gymnastics and began winning ribbons at meets. She qualified for her state's Junior Olympics, taking a fourth place on the balance beam and a third place all around. With a headband tied across her forehead and short, cropped hair, she resembled a 5'1" version of the Karate Kid.

She perfected her diving and began to teach swimming. She started writing song lyrics and made the honor roll in junior high, continuing to do so ever since. "It's not that I'm smart," she laughs. "I just try really hard. It makes up for not being really bright." She likes being an individual. A diamond glistens in one ear, and a gold fish dangles from the other.

About a year and a half after the conviction, Mercedes and her mom received a phone call from Sergeant Wally. He told them that Mr. Smith had just died in prison of a heart attack. Mercedes' mouth fell open. She stared at her mom. Sergeant Wally didn't give them any details. They wondered if the other inmates had murdered him, since prisoners rarely have any tolerance for child molesters. They would never know. The death was simply recorded as a heart attack.

That night Mercedes, her mom, and her brother ordered pizza. Mr. Smith would never be out on parole now. The ordeal was over...or so Mercedes thought.

The flashbacks began when she was 15. She remembered bits and snatches of what had happened to her so many years before. "I had blocked it out," she says. "But the flashbacks started happening more and more often. I almost went insane. I had to go back to my shrink."

"Mercedes had received a great deal of counseling from a psychologist over the years," Jane explains. "It was absolutely necessary."

Mercedes continues. "He showed me all the pictures I had drawn in therapy when I was little. They were so graphic. I had drawn everything! I couldn't believe what I had known back then, before I blocked it all out. I talked with the psychologist. He helped me. I wanted to start over fresh."

Feeling compelled to put it all down on paper again, Mercedes wrote her story in words this time instead of pictures. She felt weightless when she finished, as if she had just emptied a heavy can of trash she had been carrying around for years. She handed in her story for a school assignment on "My Most Frightening Experience."

The teacher hung her paper on the wall, keeping her name anonymous, and gave her 300 points. Only 100 points were required for an A.

"I feel better now," Mercedes says. "I'm over it." She believes that she can handle any future flashbacks as they come.

Meanwhile, Jane began working full-time for an organization called ECHO—Exploited Children's Help Organization. She started as a volunteer and was eventually hired as the coordinator. When Mercedes turned 14, she began volunteering at ECHO.

Mercedes' main function is to help other abused children through "Kids in Court," an ECHO program.

**Mercedes Jones hugs a child she has helped through "Kids in Court."**

She meets with them before they appear in court and teaches them how to testify. She explains what will happen during the trial. Often, she goes to court with them. Some children just want her near them when they're on the stand.

"There was one girl who was about my age," Mercedes says. "She had been raped by someone she went on a date with. She didn't want her mom to see the trial. She was terrified. But I went with her. We did it together. And she hugged me when it was over and told me she couldn't have done it alone.

"I tell all these children that they're heroes. Because if they don't tell their stories, the abuse won't stop. Kids who testify in court are the biggest heroes, because they save many other children. They stop some abuse.

"Sometimes I don't want to share my experience, because I'm afraid of how some people will act. But then I'm proud of what I do. I want to tell people I'm proud that I can handle this."

Mercedes will continue to share her story, because she's a survivor. Her mother agrees: "I don't think anything could stop Mercedes now."

# "THAT'S MY BIG SISTER!"

*Keema McAdoo's after-school programs keep kids off the streets and away from drugs.*

On a toasty Saturday afternoon in Ronan Park in Dorchester, Massachusetts, you might find Keema McAdoo surrounded by a knot of children. "Hey, that's my big sister, Keema!" Jimmy shouts, pointing and tugging at his grandmother's sleeve. He slips away from his grandmother's side and joins the parade of children following Keema under the tall and ancient oak trees.

Keema laughs, wraps her arms around two of the children, and tells them a story. But this isn't a story about The Three Little Pigs. It's a true story about a real person, 11-year-old Azio, who's lying in a coma at Boston City Hospital from a drug overdose.

Keema keeps the tone of her story light, but she makes her warning clear. She grins and touches the tip of Jimmy's nose. "So don't ever do drugs. Not ever!" The children laugh. Jimmy runs his hands over Keema's long, pink fingernails. Another child tugs gently at her ponytails, one at the back of her crown, the other at the nape of her neck. He unties her black ribbon.

27

Keema wasn't always popular with children. When she was in the eighth grade, she sat alone on a wooden bench in that very same park and watched the children swing. "I looked around me and saw things changing for the worse. Kids were rude to parents and teachers. There was a lot of crime and vandalism going on." She worried about her four little sisters, Nikki, Tahja, Tamara, and Judy, growing up in a community like that. She wanted to do something about it.

So she did. She joined an after-school outreach program at her middle school, Grover Cleveland, which allows kids like Keema to help out in the community. The adult leaders trained her in the dangers of drug abuse. She learned about AIDS and kids involved in violence.

"There had been a rash of violence from teens," she says. "They said they had nothing to do. So we talked to teens in the streets. They'd hang around in groups, talking loud and being rude. We tried to pull them back into the gym after school to play basketball and softball or just to jump rope."

It took time, but it worked. Bored dropouts and gang members sauntered back into the gym, their hands stuffed in the backs of their jeans, looking a little skeptical, a little unsure. But before long Keema would toss a basketball at a girl with spiked hair, challenging her to a one-on-one. Then the game would begin.

Sometimes Keema planned field trips to bowling alleys or up Butternut Mountain to ski. Kids laughed, chucked snowballs, and tackled each other. Now they had things to do and places to go. They belonged.

When Keema was a student at Jeremiah E. Burke High School, she was elected president of Student Leadership and worked with the Student Council for three years in a row. She decided that Burke needed an after-school program like the one at Grover Cleveland Middle School.

"Our school is not in the best neighborhood," she explains. "It had a pretty bad reputation." She worked with the Student Council and an adult adviser to set up the program, and she led discussions in the council meetings.

When Burke's program was off and running, another local high school, Madison Park, asked Keema to help them set up a similar program for their students. Soon Keema was speaking at other schools about drug abuse, the problems of the homeless, even how to encourage 19-year-olds to vote. She started some groups recycling and working for clean water.

But Keema never forgot how much she loved little children. She knew that the best time to teach kids to stay off drugs and do what's right is when they are young, even before they start middle school. So she organized an after-school tutoring program for children at Holland Elementary School. Twice a week, for an hour and a half each time, she and six other friends worked with more than 45 children. "We bought our own supplies," she says. "Things like books, crayons, phonics books, even snacks. And we earned the money by selling candy and flowers on Valentine's Day."

Keema first met seven-year-old Jimmy at Holland School. She was kneeling on the floor, sorting game pieces, when a pair of worn sneakers parked in front of her. The untied shoestrings straggled to the sides of his sneakers like over-cooked spaghetti. Keema looked up to see a sad, jam-smeared face.

"I can't come here," he said. The corners of his mouth drooped. "My mama won't let me."

"Why not?" Keema asked, standing up.

"Because I can't cross the street."

Keema smiled and pulled him close. She rubbed his short black curly hair. "Don't worry." She lifted his chin. "I'll call your mother, and I'll walk you home."

Keema worked with Jimmy on phonics and simple math problems. But mostly she just loved him, and walked him home each night. His teacher had told Keema that Jimmy was "wild." Soon, however, he calmed down in class. And he began calling Keema his "big sister." She became a big sister to all the children.

One day, when Keema was teaching kids at Lee Elementary about drug abuse, they had a big surprise. She and the children had been told that they would have visitors from Washington, D.C. Suddenly they heard a great rumbling in the sky outside their classroom.

The children scampered out of their seats to press their noses against the window. They saw three helicopters swoop down on Franklin Field next to the school, their giant rotors blowing the grass flat. Out hopped Massachusetts Senator Edward Kennedy, Governor Michael Dukakis, and William Bennett, Director of the Office of National Drug Control Policy. After them came a swarm of television and newspaper reporters. The officials had come to speak to the class about drug abuse. They also wanted to watch Keema in action.

It was an on-the-spot moment, and Keema felt her stomach tighten into a knot. While the officials watched, she and the children did an anti-drug role play. Then the officials spoke to the kids and zoomed back up into the sky.

Besides her work in the schools, Keema also helped her peers. She joined the Boston Against Drugs group and the Governor's Alliance for Drugs. She worked with Boston Mayor Raymond Flynn on the Violence Prevention Committee and the AIDS Prevention Committee. She helped to start a Citywide Youth Congress.

While on these committees, Keema helped other teens to combat drugs and violence. She was invited to speak at schools and community meetings, on radio and TV shows. Mostly she spoke about the teen leadership

**Keema McAdoo with Senator Ted Kennedy.** Photo courtesy U.S. Senate.

program at Burke High School. People began to respect Burke. Its reputation changed.

One time, Keema almost made a big mistake. "I went to a school, ready to give them a hard-core speech on the dangers of drugs. It was a real 'drugs-can-fry-your-brains-and-liver' speech. I got there and found out I would be talking to little third and fourth graders!" She laughs. "I had to wing it. I did a role play with them on how to refuse drugs. It worked okay. But I was pretty tense.

After that, I double-checked ahead of time where I would be going and who I would be talking to."

Keema attended a Boston Against Drugs Rally, where she gave a speech and introduced the Reverend Jesse Jackson before 15,000 people gathered around City Hall. "I was very nervous," she admits. "I had to speak for three to four minutes. But I just told all these people that no matter what anyone else says about them, they can always be the best they want to be if they believe in themselves. When we were through, the Reverend Jackson hugged me and congratulated me."

Keema spoke before so many large crowds that her big sister, Tara, began to tease her. "Keema, you can't do anything small," Tara would say. When Tara overheard Keema planning a party with her friends, she piped up, "Now, I don't want you to go and invite half the city of Boston. Just remember they wouldn't fit in our house."

Today people recognize Keema as she walks down the street. Sometimes kids ask for her autograph. Even at Boston University, where Keema is now a student, people point and sometimes whisper in awe. Keema has been called a leader, an activist—maybe a future governor.

But the thing she likes hearing most is when she walks quietly through Ronan Park beneath the tall and ancient oaks and a small voice yells, "Hey, that's Keema. She's my big sister. She taught me how to read."

# CRIME WATCHING PAYS AT SOUTHRIDGE HIGH

*When a student got shot after a basketball game, the Spartan Patrol flew into action.*

In June, 1985, a graduate of Southridge High in Miami, Florida, was standing across the street from the school when he was shot and killed. Nobody knew who did it or why. Sitting in the middle of federally-subsidized housing, the school had become a breeding ground for crime.

As a result of that senseless death, Principal Fred Rogers requested that Dr. Vic Nardelli be transferred to Southridge to set up a program to ensure greater safety in and around the school. Dr. Nardelli had already established himself as a man of action in solving crime problems in other schools.

33

Dr. Nardelli looked around Southridge and learned that the student population was one-third black, one-third white, and one-third Hispanic, Asian, and other ethnic groups. "I thought to myself, 'All kinds of kids want to belong to groups,'" Dr. Nardelli remembers. "'We'll create a positive gang that includes everyone. One that cares about ourselves and the community.'"

As soon as he was on staff at Southridge, he called the students together and announced, "This is your home. It's where you spend over half of your teenage years. Would you let someone commit crimes in your private homes? Of course not. Well, we all live here at Southridge. We're a family, and we need to take care of each other."

Southridge's Youth Crime Watch (YCW) program was born that year. Started with help from the National Crime Prevention Council in Washington, D.C., it has grown to include 2,600 out of the 2,900 students at the school, plus all the faculty members, administrators, secretaries, parents, cafeteria workers, and maintenance personnel. With so many members, YCW boasts that it has become the largest anti-crime organization in the nation.

The central power of YCW is the Spartan Patrol, an organization of 75 YCW members including honor students, football players, former dropouts, and former drug users. Wearing red badges on their chests, the leaders patrol hallways, parking lots, and bathrooms between classes and during lunch periods. If they see a rule breaker, a Spartan Patroller will casually remind the offender, "I'm sorry, but would you mind picking that up?" Or, "Excuse me, but you'll have to walk the other way down this hall. You know we have a one-way system."

The program works on positive peer pressure and anonymous tips delivered to Dr. Nardelli or any other administrator. Students can drop tips in their mailboxes, slip them under Dr. Nardelli's door, or walk into his office in person. If a problem persists after a student is warned, the Spartan Patroller immediately reports it. Two resident police officers, Officer Cheryl Wiggins of the Miami Metro Police and Officer Nelson Santos of the School Resource Police, investigate the anonymous tips from Youth Crime Watchers.

Student Barbara Castro is president of Youth Crime Watch. She is also vice president of the senior class. As a student leader, she has helped to organize pep rallies against crime. "'Power 96,' a popular radio station, came over and ran a pep rally for us," she says. "We had a band. The kids really liked it. We hold a lot of assemblies like that."

Barbara lives with her mother, Maria, who has an incurable disease and can't work. "You know, I used to be really shy," Barbara explains. "When I was in elementary and junior high, I was terrified to speak in front of people. My voice would shake, and I'd just mumble. Now I love talking to the student body."

Barbara straightens her black T-shirt with its Spartan Patrol monogram. "We wear these every Wednesday," she says. "We really have solved crimes, too.

"Last year, one of our students, Lazaro Gutierrez, was sitting in his car in the school parking lot after a football game, waiting for his girlfriend. She was a cheerleader. It was around 10:00 to 10:30 at night. In the back of the school is this pretty bad neighborhood called The Project. Well, a couple of kids from The Project came over and hassled Lazaro and asked him for his wallet. He said no. And they just kept harassing him. Lazaro hit the gas to get out of there, and one guy from The Project pulled out a gun and shot Lazaro in the neck. Lazaro didn't die, but he's paralyzed now.

"On Monday morning after the shooting, Dr. Nardelli announced to all the students, 'We have got to pull together to find out who did this.' That same day, about

20 different clues came in from students. Some of them had been at the game. With all those tips, our school police were able to arrest those guys from The Project."

Barbara pauses in the school corridor to answer a question from another YCW member. She steps forward and points, encouraging him to patrol in another hall. She's 5'9", attractive, and walks with poise. She hopes to become a model someday.

Barbara returns. "There have been other times when YCW has caught lawbreakers," she says. "For example, we got to school one day and found graffiti all over the outside of the building. Dr. Nardelli made an announcement again. 'We need to know who did this.' he said. 'Who painted our house?' He always goes on like that. We're one big family here. He said, 'Crime Watch people are not snitchers. You wouldn't call it snitching if you reported someone who defaced your private home. This is no different.'

"He made that announcement at 8:00 in the morning. By 10:00, just two hours later, the police had arrested the kids. That was because of all the clues that poured in again from Crime Watchers." She lowers her voice. "You know, some of our group are former gang members, and they let us in on all the things gang members do."

Sandy St. Amand is president of the Spartan Patrol. She is also president of the senior class. Walking swiftly, with her head held high, she appears to be unafraid of anything. The school faculty and staff appointed both Barbara and Sandy.

"One day I went into Dr. Nardelli's office, and I told him I would like to be in Spartan Patrol," Sandy remembers. "He said maybe I could, and would I like to be president, too?" Her voice squeaks as she laughs. "Dr. Nardelli is just like a father. He's so loving and caring. Words can't express how I feel about him. I love that man.

**Barbara Castro (L), Dr. Vic Nardelli, and Sandra St. Amand meet to discuss Youth Crime Watch.** Photo courtesy of the Southridge High photo staff.

"But I get along with everybody. I love peer counseling. I like to help people with personal problems as well as academics. I'm in love with the telephone."

Sandy isn't shy about intervening on a problem-in-progress. "If I see a fight brewing, I find some way to prevent it," she says. "Sometimes it's not even on campus. Spartan Patrol goes into the community, too.

"A while back, I was sitting with my mom at a restaurant in our local mall. As I was about to order, I heard this mumbling behind me. I turned around and saw these two groups of kids arguing over a girl. They were ready to fight.

"I marched into the center of them and said, 'Hey, what's going on? You don't need to do this.' Some of the students were from Southridge, and some were from another high school. One guy on each side had been dating this girl, and they were ready to fight it out. Immature stuff.

"A Southridge guy said, 'You may be president of Spartan Patrol, but this is not school-related. Let that stay in our school.'

"I said, 'Spartan Patrol isn't just about our school. It's also about our community. I'm not going to stand up here and watch you guys fight over nonsense like this. It's not going to be done here.'

"The two groups broke up and went their separate ways. It's funny, but I wasn't afraid. I knew the guys from my school. They're not the type of people to fight. I know all the students. They won't pull tricks on me. They respect the Spartan Patrol."

Sandy lives with her father, Fred, who came from Haiti when he was only 14, and her mother, Leura, a nurse. She has an older brother and a little sister. Her father, who is chairman of Miami's Little Haiti Subcouncil for Crime Prevention, says of Sandy, "She's a one-of-a-kind person. Very outspoken. Very intelligent. She does what she wants. She can talk to anybody. She's ready for the real world."

What does Sandy want in the real world? She plans to go to Howard University to study political science and maybe get a law degree. "And I'm sort of committed to one guy. He's a year older and plays football for the University of Miami Hurricanes."

Sandy and the Spartan Patrol have received support from state lawmakers. The Florida Legislature passed a law which states that selling, distributing, or handling drugs within 1,000 feet of any school is punishable with

a mandatory three-year prison sentence. Anyone trespassing on Southridge School grounds will quickly be
reported by Crime Watchers.

What has the YCW accomplished? Today there are
very few fights and virtually no bicycle chain snatchings
(a crime in which someone riding a bike rips a chain
necklace from a victim's neck). The school has a low
truancy rate. Kids don't hide drugs in lockers or try to
sell them in bathrooms or between classes anymore—not
with 2,600 pairs of eyes watching.

"In the three years that I've been here," Sandy says,
"I haven't ever seen an incident where someone was
arrested for drugs in our school. We don't have a drug
problem here. I don't expect to see one. We wouldn't
allow it in our home."

# DREAMS, THREATS, AND SWEATY PALMS

*Norvell Smith knew there would be gang members in the audience. But she looked right at them and gave them a piece of her mind.*

When Norvell Smith was seven years old, she often sneaked off into the woods by the local high school to be alone. After gathering an armful of yellow and white daisies, she would nestle down under a tall oak tree in a secluded spot. In this secret place, Norvell was freed from breathing the black haze that belched into the air from the factory smokestacks near her Chicago housing unit. There were no gangs, no yelling, only the whistling of cardinals—*tsip, tsip*.

Sometimes she pulled out a crumpled piece of paper, bit off the end of a broken pencil lead, and wrote poetry. She wrote about her dad. What did he look like? Did she resemble him? What was he

41

doing right then? She could only imagine, because she had never met her father.

She wrote about her mother, Willie, who was a waitress and a cook, and her older sister, Linda, who mostly raised them. They were five girls, Norvell, Linda, Doris, Anita, and Janice, and two boys, Jimmy and Eric. She wrote nice things about her family. They stuck together.

Then Norvell would fall back into the pillow of daisies and shut her eyes. Her father had been a good speaker, her mother had told her. Norvell imagined herself as a speaker, too—standing in front of crowds, holding their attention with her words. She wondered what she would say. Maybe she would say things that would help other people. Maybe everyone would listen to her.

As Norvell grew older, the gang violence increased in her Union Street neighborhood, with its rows of single-family houses.

"Starting when I was in sixth grade, high school gang members would come over to our school, John Hope School, and shoot around at the kids," she remembers. "Nobody did anything. They were shooting at other gang members. We were all scared to death. Within a ten-year period, twenty children were killed because of gang violence."

One day, after the school science fair, a young eighth-grade gang member decided he wanted to cross over Garfield Boulevard to McDonald's to buy some fries. "Even though he was a gang member, everyone liked him," Norvell says. "My friend Latisha used to call him 'Everyday,' because he usually wore the same pants to school every day."

His friends warned him not to cross over, because that meant he would be entering another gang's turf. But Everyday went over anyway. He got his fries, but when he came out of McDonald's, a rival gang member shot Everyday in the head and killed him.

"It really made everyone upset," Norvell says, sliding her glasses along her nose. "But that wasn't all.
There were more crimes. My friend's sister ran away
from home one day. She was pregnant and hid in the
basement of an old abandoned building. A gang found
her and beat her up, and then they killed her and her
baby. She wasn't even a gang member. But one of the
boys that beat her up was the one that got her pregnant.
No one even found her until days later."

And then there was a boy named Charles, who was
only 13 years old. One day his brother didn't pick him
up from school. Charles made the mistake of walking
down the boulevard with a gang member to pass time.
A boy from a rival gang hollered from across the street.
Charles's friend couldn't accept the taunting and ran
across to shoot it out with his rival. Although Charles
remained on his side of the street, a bullet ricocheted
and hit Charles in the back. He died instantly.

"He didn't even get to graduate," Norvell says,
clenching her fist. "Almost all us kids in the school went
to his funeral. The killing was drug-related. Where
there are gangs, there are drugs. But the gang members,
they don't use drugs. They don't want to get addicted.
They just sell them."

Norvell rolls back her black eyes. "One time
I almost got killed myself. I was late out of school, and
the bus had already left. I was walking outside of the
school. I heard shots and saw some boys shooting.

"We're adapted to this. It happens all the time. We
just hide and wait for the shooting to stop and then go on
with our regular life when it's over. So I ran over behind
this light pole and waited. When the shooting stopped,
I looked around and ran for the bus stop. I got to the bus
stop, and this shot whizzed right by my waist.

"I fell to the ground and crawled behind a gray
Chevy. And then I looked up and saw a boy ten steps

behind me. The bullet skinned his stomach, and he fell to the ground. I was in shock. I stood up and saw the security guards from the school rushing over. I don't remember if I saw anyone else. I just caught the bus and got out of there and went home.

"My mom said I shouldn't go back to John Hope School, but I wanted to. My friends were all there."

Finally many of the parents got fed up with the violence. They picketed the school, carrying signs demanding better protection for their children. The children avoided the TV cameras that followed the story, fearful that gang members would get them if they said anything against gangs.

"It was the first time I saw parents doing something about the violence," Norvell says. "Their protest didn't do any good, but we had always wanted them to do something against gangs. Most of the kids are raised by grandparents, or a grandmother, or a single parent. The kids do what they want most of the time."

Then Project Serve arrived at John Hope and changed Norvell's life forever. Police officers organized the project and taught students about drugs, gangs, violence, and AIDS. They announced a speech contest. The best speech would win a medal.

When Norvell heard the announcement about the speech contest, her chest burned inside her. Although the thought frightened her, she knew she was going to write one of those speeches. She knew she had to. She would go to her sisters, Janice and Anita, to ask for advice on writing her speech.

Fifty kids from John Hope acted as the judges for the speech contest. Only ten kids had the courage to speak. Norvell was one of them. And of the ten speakers, Norvell was chosen as one of the three finalists.

Later, she found a note pushed through the vent in her locker. It said simply, "You'd better shat your mouth." Norvell laughed. Whoever wrote the note didn't even know how to spell "shut."

It hadn't been too hard to speak before a select group of 50 kids. But when Norvell learned that the three finalists would have to speak before the entire school—all 950 students—she almost swallowed her tongue.

On the day of her speech, Norvell recalls, "I was afraid of being booed, or getting things thrown at me. All the gang members would be in the audience. I was afraid of what might happen after school. What would I do? Should I run for the bus or ask my teacher to take me home? My mother couldn't get off work to listen to my speech. I had no one with me. I only had my teacher."

The more Norvell thought about it, the more her stomach flipped around. Her palms grew sweaty. Her cheeks felt hot. Should she back out? It wasn't too late yet. Everyone would forgive her, and probably congratulate her.

The other two students spoke first. One spoke about drugs, and the other talked about interpersonal violence. Their speeches were good, but not especially earth-shaking.

Then Norvell heard her name called. Her heart skipped. For a second, she remembered lying in a bed of daisies, dreaming of making a speech. Then her mind forced her back to the auditorium of John Hope. She pushed her feet underneath her body. Somebody had to speak out. Someone had to have the guts to call a halt to gangs.

She stared at two teachers. They smiled and seemed to say, "Go on. You can do it." Norvell stood up. She left her fear lying there in the auditorium seat, like a shed skin. She spoke into the microphone with a steady voice for five whole minutes.

"I'm sick and tired of every time I come out of this building getting shot at, harassed, beat on.... We really want things safe for all the kids....The only thing you can get from a gang is a hole in the head or six feet under. Take your choice. Either way, you end up dead...."

And then Norvell noticed the two thousand eyes staring at her. It was so quiet that the whole audience seemed to be holding its breath. She looked straight at gang members and went on talking, meaning every word.

"Your parents have so much hope for you. What are you doing? The best way to get out of this is to get a good education. It's your only passport out of this neighborhood...."

Norvell finished. There was a pause, and then the clapping began. It grew louder. Kids stood up and cheered. She looked out at the white eyes, the white teeth, the smiles. And she swallowed a thickness in her throat. "I looked at a gang member, Steve. He smiled at me."

**Norvell Smith gets hugs after her speech.** Photo courtesy of Norvell Smith.

The applause grew louder. The kids clapped and cheered for five minutes. "I felt like I had just saved the whole world," Norvell says.

She was handed a gold medal. Soon TV and newspaper reporters surrounded her for interviews. Her story was flashed around the state and the nation. Norvell received hundreds of letters from other children who said, "It's time someone stood up."

As a result of the attention Norvell's speech received, police started patrolling the school. They were everywhere: in front of the building, behind the building, in the halls, on the boulevard. John Hope was safe. There were no more shootings. Suddenly John Hope became a famous school, a good school.

Norvell has continued giving speeches. Not only has she spoken at many elementary schools, but she has also addressed principals, college presidents, and business people to gain support for Project Serve.

When Norvell started ninth grade at Dunbar High School, she went to her new principal and asked about passing a petition to collect names from other kids who were against gang violence. Her principal told her to wait until things cooled down a little. Now Norvell is working on starting "Youth Speakers Speaking for the Truth." Young people will visit other schools and warn them against gang violence and drugs.

In 1990, Norvell received a surprise phone call from the Giraffe Project, a non-profit organization that honors people who "stick their necks out" and act courageously to serve the common good. Someone had told them about Norvell and how she had spoken out against gang violence. The Giraffe Project wanted to give her an award for her courage. When she heard this, Norvell cried. She never imagined that all this could happen to her.

Norvell's award was a trip to the Soviet Union, where she met Andy Holleman and other young people

who had taken risks to make a difference in the world.
(You can read Andy Holleman's story on pages 143–150.)
She spoke to Soviet students, telling them about the life
of an African-American in Chicago, about the drugs,
about violence, and about how even one person can take
a stand.

The Soviet students, halfway around the world from
John Hope School, were a lot like the kids back home.
They listened to the speech.  And then they, too, stood
up and applauded Norvell Smith, a great speaker.

# KIDS TAKING SOCIAL ACTION

*W*hat's social action?  It is not *getting a date with your ultimate hunk or dreamgirl.  Although that's nice, too, social action in this book means all those unselfish contributions you make to other people in your community.  If you spend hours reading to the blind, organizing dances for senior citizens, or passing a petition to gain representation on your school board, you are taking social action.  Simple things count, too—like sharing some of your clothing and toys with a needy child.*

*You don't serve others to gain personal rewards.  You do it because you care about other people and want to make the world a better place.  Still, you get a rush up the back of your neck when a 90-year-old lady smiles because you sang her favorite song.  You can't help feeling proud when you report to your school board on how to ban the use of plastics in the school lunch program.  And it's wonderful to see a lonely child clutch your favorite old teddy bear to his chest.*

*Giving to and caring for others makes you happy, and it helps others and the community.  But that's not all it does.  Reaching out to help also helps you.  The skills you learn enable you to take more control of your own life.  You get better at setting goals and making decisions.  You gain self-confidence and self-esteem.  Then you don't have to depend on others to tell you that you're great.  You already know it!*

*You're about to meet several young people who have made social action part of their lives.  Like Joby Shimomura, who fights for kids' rights.  And Jenna and Rena Duncan, young Native Americans who convinced lawmakers to put name plates on two sculptures.  (You'll find out why.)  And Samuel Long, who devotes hours to helping disabled children.  Finally, you'll get to know Frank Daily, who reached out to help a stranger.*

*These kids have all done remarkable things.  So can you.*

# 10 TIPS
# FOR TAKING SOCIAL ACTION

## 1. Choose a problem.

Look around your neighborhood. Are there any places that need attention (scraggly landscapes, broken sidewalks, empty lots where trash collects)? Are there places where you don't feel safe? Places that smell funny? Are there homeless people, hungry children, problems with drugs? Pick one problem to work on.

## 2. Do your research.

Find out everything you can about your problem. Magazines and newspapers are good places to start looking. But try telephoning for ideas, writing letters, and interviewing people. Talk to your neighbors and other kids in your school. You can even talk to city or state officials. The more you know about your problem, the better your chances are of solving it.

## 3. Think of many possible solutions to your problem.

Sometimes the craziest ideas turn out to be the best. You can choose one solution, or you might try many different approaches. Remember to be polite and kind at all times, even with people who don't agree with you. You want to *solve* problems, not *become* a problem for others.

## 4. Build a strong support team.

Find all the people who agree with your ideas. Survey your neighborhood, school, newspapers, city officials, and everyone else you can think of. The more people you have on your team, the more power you will have to make a difference.

## 5. Identify your opposition.

In other words, find out all the people who might try to throw tacks in your path. Search out those who disagree with your solution. Talk with them. Tell them your ideas. If you include them, they might decide to help you instead of oppose you. And you might discover places where you can compromise or change your mind a little.

## 6. Advertise.

Did you know that TV, radio, and newspaper reporters love stories about kid action? And TV and radio stations usually offer free air time for good causes. But don't forget small community newspapers, even church bulletins. When you let others know what you are trying to do, all sorts of people will join your team.

## 7. Raise money for your cause, if you think it might help.

People often listen to you more when you raise money for your plan. Even if you only collect a small amount, this shows that you are serious about wanting to solve your problem.

## 8. Carry out your solutions.

You have lined up your team players, and you've advertised to inform others of your problem and solution. Now DO IT! Make a list of all the steps you need to take. Give speeches, write letters, pass petitions, improve your own neighborhood, campaign for world peace (or you might just try to spiff up your own backyard).

## 9. Evaluate your progress.

Is your plan working or not? Are you congratulating yourself, or do you have a huge headache? Either way, it's time to re-examine your project. Do you need to try something different? Find more people

to help?  Change your idea?  Be honest with yourself, then do what needs to be done.

## 10. Don't give up.

Don't pay too much attention to those people who
will tell you all the reasons why your solution won't
work.  If you think your cause is important, keep
picking away at it.  Problem-solving means weeding
out all the things that don't work until you find
something that does.

Remember, a mountain looks tallest from the
bottom.  Don't give up.  Climb!

---

Adapted from "Ten Tips for Taking Social Action" by Barbara A. Lewis, in
THE KID'S GUIDE TO SOCIAL ACTION (Free Spirit Publishing Inc., 1991).

# HONORING THEIR ANCESTORS

*To Rena and Jenna Duncan, those statues in the Capitol Building weren't just two anonymous Indians. They were John Duncan and Unca Som.*

Rena and Jenna Duncan live about a mile apart, down dusty roads skirted with sagebrush and tall grass, nestled at the base of the Uintah Mountains in Utah. They ride horses past cedar trees and beneath low-hanging willows, over the 39 acres of pasture land surrounding Rena's white frame house. They keep all kinds of pets: dogs, cats, hamsters, whatever wanders by.

From their names, you might think they are sisters, maybe even twins. They're not. Rena is Jenna's aunt—her mother's sister—and Jenna is Rena's niece. But the two girls have grown up together like sisters. On a weekend evening, you might find them giggling together in their sleeping bags on Rena's bedroom carpet, pretending to be asleep. Rena makes up ghost stories to try to scare Jenna, who covers her head with her pillow to smother her laughter.

They're regular Native American girls. Jenna likes rap music and is a bit of a tease. She hopes to become a doctor or veterinarian someday. She's friendly and good at math.

Rena likes to draw cartoons and write stories, which she keeps locked in her secret journal. Because she is fascinated by the Anasazi Indian culture, she dreams of becoming an anthropologist.

Both girls enjoy reading mysteries. School is not hard for them. But it wasn't always that way for Rena. When Rena started kindergarten, she hated to go into the strange place where she didn't know everybody. "I'm shy until I get to know people," she admits. "Then I talk a lot."

Rena and Jenna were among the first Native American children to attend the formerly all-white Neola Elementary School. At first, school was a struggle for Rena. Instead of listening to the teacher, she would gaze out the window and imagine that she was with her father, examining an ancient Anasazi ruin.

Rena's father, Clifford Duncan, is Director of the Museum for the Ute Indian Tribe. He often shows archaeologists how to identify historical sites and remains. "I respect my dad because he knows a lot and helps me to understand the world better," Rena says.

She loves tromping along with her dad on explorations. Sometimes she stops to gather bluebells from mountain cliffs. She studies petroglyphs—drawings on cave walls—and asks, "Who drew these pictures? What were they trying to say?" Her dad weaves stories of ancient ancestors and explains what he thinks the strange little stick figures mean.

Once Rena saw a half-buried arrowhead in the dirt. As she reached down to snatch it, her father caught her by the wrist. "Rena, whenever you take something from the place that ancient people lived, you must leave something

in return," he told her. "Then you are not just taking."
His dark eyes held her in check, but they twinkled.

Rena pulled a red scarf from her hair and laid it on
the dirt, smoothing out the corners. Her dad prayed to
the ancient ones to accept the exchange. He nodded at
Rena, and only then did she pick up the arrowhead.

Clifford finds other treasures in the hills. When
Rena is sick, he climbs the Uintah foothills to collect
sagebrush and bitter herbs for medicinal tea, which he
prepares for her. Once a doctor gave her penicillin, but
that made her worse. She prefers her father's tea.

Rena takes part in many Indian ceremonies performed by her father. The ancient sweat ceremonies are
only for the family. Together, they sing, pray, and inhale
steam from the hot rocks. In the summer, Rena watches
Clifford participate in the Sundance Ceremony, fasting
for three or four days and nights to cleanse his mind and
body, communicating with the Creator, and renewing his
attachment to the spirit of the world and of nature.
During that ceremony, Rena sings with the women and
imagines the different roles the animals played in the
creation of the world.

Sometimes Rena watches over her dad's shoulder,
his black braids trailing down his back, as he paints pictures. One of her favorites shows the opening of the
earth at creation, with birds flying out. She watches
Clifford dip his paintbrush into somber grays, browns,
and deep blue acrylics. She imagines how the world
must have been at the very beginning, with all of nature
singing together. She is proud that one of her father's
paintings hangs in the Smithsonian Institution in
Washington, D.C.

In spite of Rena's creative imagination, grade school
remained a struggle for her. Nothing seemed to sink in
or make sense. She didn't understand the strange sym-
bols which stood for words. Arithmetic numbers danced

around the page, refusing to stand still, as she pretended they were tiny animals.

Finally, in the fourth grade, a teacher named Mrs. Luck "turned the light on for her and brought her out," says Rena's mother, Charlene. Mrs. Luck saw strong talent in Rena. Noticing that Rena was interested in archaeology, Mrs. Luck encouraged her to enter the history fair. Suddenly school made sense to Rena. She won prizes in the fair several years in a row.

Shortly after fourth grade, Rena's dad took her to the Utah State Capitol Building in Salt Lake City. He had something important to show her. He took her to the House of Representatives and pointed to two white marble busts—statues showing the upper part of the body—at the entrance to the House chambers.

**John Duncan (L) and Unca Som, after their name plates were added.**
Photos courtesy of *Ute Bulletin*.

Rena saw that the busts were of Native American men.  When she looked closer, she recognized one as John Duncan, her own great-great grandfather.  She held her breath and looked at the other.  It was Unca Som, her great-great-great grandfather!  Her black eyes grew larger.  She stood and stared.

Then she noticed something else—something that wasn't there.  Neither statue had a name plate.

Rena calculated.  For 50 years, those sculptures had watched over legislators as they bustled past, while lobbyists pressed for laws and amendments.  To most people, they were just two anonymous sculptures of American Indians.  But if you stopped to look at them, you could see the wrinkles at the corners of John Duncan's kind eyes, his long braids, a hint of a smile on Unca Som's face.  These were stone portraits of real men.

Rena's father spoke to her of Unca Som, the medicine man.  During the winter, Clifford said, "he'd chop wood in the snow for the stove.  He would wear no shoes, because his belief was so strong, and the cold would not affect him."

He also spoke of John Duncan, the last great chief of the Uintah Band.  As a delegate for the tribe, John Duncan had traveled to Washington, D.C., in leadership capacities.  "He had many friends with Sioux, Shoshone, Navajos, and white people, too," Clifford explained.  "Everyone respected the Indian leader on the great white horse.  People came to trade buckskins for rugs or just to talk with John Duncan."

And then Rena's dad reminded her that she had been born in the Heber Valley.  So had John Duncan.  "There is a connection between you two," her mother often said.

Sometimes Rena felt that connection with the past.  When she made up stories so scary that she even frightened herself, gazing about her bedroom at the black night shadows, she would suddenly feel the ancient ones watching over her.  Then she would fall asleep in a sweep of peace.

Her link to John Duncan would grow even stronger. When Rena and Jenna were in sixth grade, Mr. Dallas Murray, a fifth-grade teacher at nearby Myton Elementary, contacted the girls.  He expressed concern over the fact that no name plates identified the busts of their ancestors at the Capitol building.  Mr. Murray had grown up near the Ute Indian Reservation.  He recognized Unca Som and John Duncan each time he took his own class to the State Legislature.

Mr. Murray suggested that they all go to the Utah Legislature to propose a resolution to put name plates on the sculptures.  The girls could testify for the resolution on the floor of the House of Representatives, he explained.  Rena and Jenna exchanged excited grins. They ran home and grabbed paper and pencils to begin composing their speeches.

**Rena (speaking) and Jenna Duncan at the Utah State Capitol.**

When the day approached, Rena and Jenna fussed with their hair and chewed on their nails. They felt as if teams of horses were romping in their stomachs. The whole family traveled to Salt Lake City to hear the girls' speeches.

Rena and Jenna climbed the wide marble staircase to the entrance of the State Capitol. Rena felt small as she walked between tall Greek columns and into the

# JENNA DUNCAN'S TESTIMONY AT THE STATE CAPITOL

My name is Jenna Duncan, and I give the following as my testimony.

Unca Som was related to the Duncans on my Grandfather's Mother's side of the family, who are of the Whiteriver Band. He was an Indian medicine man who lived a very simple life. He resided on the Uintah Reservation since the Meeker Massacre, when the Whiterivers were placed there. He was believed to have been the oldest Indian that ever lived on the reservation.

He was known only as "Unca Som," which meant "Red Som." The name "Som" has no real meaning.

Little is known about Unca Som, because when you are a medicine man, you live only within the nature side of life, and the outside world has little meaning. To Indians, he was a man of the "Old Way of Life," because today we no longer have these true medicine men.

Being a descendant of this man gives me honor to give this testimony.

Thank you.

# RENA DUNCAN'S TESTIMONY
# AT THE STATE CAPITOL

My name is Rena Duncan, and I give the following as my testimony.

My Great-Great Grandfather, John Duncan, was born in Heber Valley around the year 1857. He was born a Tumpanawach Ute, which is part of the Uintah Band as it is known today....When the Government opened more of the Uintah Reservation to homesteading, my Great-Great Grandfather, John Duncan, was one of the delegates to travel to Washington, D.C. He also served on several other delegations to Washington, D.C. and New York on behalf of his Indian people.

Before the Indian Reorganization Act, when the Ute Indian Tribe set up their formal government system which is used today, the Utes had representatives from each band that were considered chiefs. My Great-Great Grandfather was the chief of the Uintah Band. He remained chief in 1937 although nearly blind. He died in September of 1941 and was buried in the Red Cedar Buttes in Farm Creek near Whiterocks, Utah.

My Great-Great Grandfather John Duncan was an Indian with traditional beliefs who loved his Indian people and was a friend to the non-Indian.

Even though I never knew him, he gives me pride and dignity to be an Indian, and I am honored to give this testimony on behalf of Great-Great Grandfather John Duncan.

Thank you.

huge, domed lobby.  A busload of fifth graders from
Myton and Neola Elementary schools had come to give
their support.  The thought of speaking in front of all
those kids made the girls extra nervous.  "I was afraid I'd
mess up," Jenna remembers.  Rena just waited in silence.

But as they stood to present their testimonies, the
House of Representatives grew quiet.  Fifth-grade children
from two elementary schools sat still and listened.  The
legislators stopped their bustle and listened.  Television
and newspaper reporters listened while the high ceilings
bounced back echoes of two small girls' voices.

Their voices gathered strength as they rang out their
message:  Respect Unca Som and John Duncan.  Notice
them.  Respect the heritage they contributed.  Don't
leave their sculptures nameless.

House Concurrent Resolution 7 passed both the
Utah House and Senate without one vote against it.  And
on January 16, 1990, Mr. Murray helped the girls to hang
up the name plates.  The two sculptures weren't anonymous anymore.

The following July, Rena received another surprise.
She was selected to represent the State of Utah in the
Native American Boy Scouts and Girl Scouts competition
in Boca Raton, Florida.  There she told folk tales, like
"The Coyote and Its Reflection," and performed the traditional Bear Dance and War Dance.  For the dances, she
wore beaded moccasins, a bone necklace, and a red-and-
blue native costume her mother had made from trade
cloth and shells.

As Rena danced with slow, graceful movements, the
bone necklace swayed.  Her braids, wound in otterskin
wraps, glistened.  The once shy girl then answered many
questions with poise and ease.  She wasn't the least bit
afraid.  After all, she had spoken before the Utah State

Legislature!  Rena was named a runner-up in this national competition.

When you ask her where she got her courage, Rena says, "I learned a lot about my elders as I researched and prepared my speech for the legislature.  I learned to respect Unca Som and John Duncan.  I felt pride inside. I felt pride and dignity to be an Indian.  It was an honor to do such a thing.  And now I'm not so nervous speaking before people.  I'm not so afraid now."

# FIGHTING FOR KIDS' RIGHTS

*Joby Shimomura knew that kids had something to say... if adults would only listen.*

"Fair fares for youth! Fair fares for youth!" Thirty-five teenagers chanted and carried protest signs as they rallied around the city offices in downtown Seattle, Washington. Inside, the members of the city's Metropolitan Council were holding a hearing. Outside, fifteen-year-old Joby Shimomura encouraged the teens to fight for their rights.

Everybody knew who Joby was. As the leader of the campaign to lower bus fares for young people, she had organized the demonstration. Now she spoke before the group.

"The handicapped and senior citizens get lower rates," she proclaimed. "We want bus fares lowered for kids, too! Some families don't have cars. Kids have to use the bus." Reporters scrambled for good positions for their cameras as adults and teens shouted heated words at each other.

Carrying their placards, the teens marched together to the council hearing. They were stopped abruptly at the door. "If we lower the fares for young people, we'll have to hike up senior fares," council members told them.

"That's not right," Joby responded. "You're pitting the young against the old. We never intended higher fares for seniors as a tradeoff."

Soon, newspapers printed headlines like, "Youth Stealing Grandparents' Grocery Money." Joby remembers, "It wasn't fair. As young people, we didn't have much credibility. We lost that battle."

Joby is eighteen now, and much wiser from many social-action campaigns. "We got burned out over bus fares," she continues. "But we learned a lot. One of the problems is getting people to recognize us as important. It's difficult, because there is no history of kids doing this. But we did educate the public, and we showed them that young people can organize and speak out."

What kind of girl starts a city-wide campaign to lower bus fares for kids? Joby describes herself as "pretty average." She's the middle child in her family, with a younger sister, Yoko, and an older brother, Mark. "We are all independent and outgoing," Joby says proudly. She greatly respects her parents. Her father, Roger Shimomura, is an art professor at the University of Kansas. Her mother, Bea Kiyohara, is an assistant dean of students at Seattle Central Community College, and artistic director of the Northwest Asian-American Theater. (Joby's parents are divorced.)

Joby loved elementary and middle school, but she wasn't excited by high school, which she found "boring" and "not challenging." She generated some excitement as editor of her high-school newspaper, but she often skipped classes to attend public meetings and rallies.

"Some teachers hated it when I questioned their methods of teaching through reading and taking tests,"

**Joby Shimomura speaks out for rights for kids.** Photo courtesy of Dean Wong, International Examiner.

she recalls. "But I learn better by discussing and through experiencing and doing."

When she was younger, Joby tried piano for a few years, then violin for one year, and she even sang in a choir. Those things didn't excite her, either.

In elementary school, she enjoyed sports. "But I hated it when the P.E. teacher — who was usually a man — would say, 'Oh, I'll be on the girls' team to help you out.' I'd toss the ball at him and shout, 'We don't need you!'"

In fifth grade, Joby was one of only three girls on the flag-football team. Darting in between the bigger, heavier boys, she would race down the field carrying the football. She didn't score many touchdowns, but her team won the Community Center Championship. Years later, in high school, she played varsity basketball, pitting her 5'5" frame against 5'10" opponents.

Joby makes friends easily, and she has never been afraid to try new ideas. In sixth grade, when the other girls were still wearing jeans and tennis shoes, Joby donned preppy Bermuda shorts and penny loafers. Two years later, the Bermuda fad hit, and boys started wearing them, too.

In eighth grade at Whitman Middle School, Joby was elected student body president. Meanwhile, she heard about Kidsboard, a new youth leadership group being sponsored by Seattle's Metro Center YMCA. Its purpose was to give kids a way to give advice to adults. Finally, here was something that excited Joby.

She applied and was one of 25 young people accepted into the group. As a Kidsboard member, Joby could speak out on issues that affected young people. "We see things no one else can really see," she often said. "They're not our age."

When local authorities proposed a curfew for teenagers, Joby and the other Kidsboard members protested. "We decided there was no fair way to enforce the idea. We testified at community hearings and before the city council." Joby arranged for a press conference to explain the Kidsboard position on the issue. She helped write the Kidsboard testimony against the curfew. And this time, adults listened. The curfew was defeated.

Joby and Kidsboard didn't always succeed. When the city council decided to shut down Seattle's teen dance clubs, the kids fought back, but they won only part of that battle.

The city had already banned cruising at a local beach after residents complained. Now they wanted to close a half-dozen dance clubs that had served as hangouts for teens. Their reason? Council members stated that the dance halls encouraged problems with drug use, violence, and sex.

But the teens needed someplace to stomp their feet and feel the beat of music thumping in their chests. "I testified before city council to keep the halls open, but to regulate them," Joby says. "If you close the dance halls, you have groups hanging out somewhere else. They get bored and restless." Joby further told the council, "When you talk about issues and leave out young people, then it doesn't make sense. There's a hole in the picture." A couple of the dance clubs stayed open, but not all. And they're regulated now.

Joby gestures wildly with her hands as she speaks. She looks down at her palms and laughs. "My friends tell me that if they were ever to tie my hands behind my back, I couldn't talk. I think they're right."

She realizes that social action doesn't always mean winning. For example, when she lobbied the legislature to try to get funding for children's programs, she was unsuccessful. "Leadership doesn't always mean you get what you want," she observes. "You need to experience what it feels like to *not* get what you want, to fail. You need to fall to experience how to get up for the next time."

Overall, Joby has succeeded more times than she has failed. When she turned seventeen, she became one of the key planners for the second annual Teen Convention. A Kidsboard project, the convention focused on youth violence. Around 200 young people attended from many area high schools.

Joby also worked the Teen Hotline, another Kidsboard idea funded by the Metro Center YMCA. Troubled teens can dial the Hotline and talk about their problems with other young people. They call with questions on teen pregnancy, drug abuse, suicide, and health concerns. Sometimes they just want to know how to get along better with their friends.

"I remember once I talked with someone who had breast cancer," Joby says. "She didn't know how to tell her family. She was confused and scared. I talked with her and listened. Later, she called back and wanted to become a volunteer. She had told her parents and was happy with her decision. We get a lot of 'thanks-a-lot' calls. It makes me feel absolutely wonderful. It makes the training worthwhile."

When Norm Rice, a city council member, decided to run for mayor, Joby helped him to campaign. Rice designated her as an area coordinator. "I was the 'rah-rah' person who made sure that sign-wavers for Rice were visible at Seattle Sea Hawks football games, University of Washington Huskies games, parades, and other big events," she explains. She phoned voters and hit the pavement door-to-door for five intensive months. When Rice won, he hired her to work for him in the mayor's office.

Joby's list of accomplishments reads almost like a congressional leader's. She has spent more time in law-making chambers than a lot of legislators. She has testified for youth before city government and at the Washington state legislature. From 1986 to 1990, she even testified before congressional committees in Washington, D.C., where she told the nation's legislators that youth should be utilized as a valuable resource, and that adults need to hear from young people about decisions that affect them. She later appeared with Senator Ted Kennedy on the *Today Show* to discuss these issues.

One of Joby's dreams is to get at least two young people on every city board and commission in Seattle—health, the arts, animal control, everything. And she wants them there not merely as advisers, but as *voting* members.

Joby left Seattle in 1991 to fly to Washington, D.C., where she has worked as an assistant to U.S. Congressman John Miller. She wants to go to college, probably to study public relations. But she does plan to stay in public service as an advocate for children.

Joby stretches out her hands. "You know, I'm really lucky, because I have found my passion."

Donna James, Special Assistant to Mayor Rice, has high praise for Joby Shimomura. "She has devoted years of her life to making sure the voices of young people are being heard throughout our city, and has managed to bring the message to both the state and national levels. Some people say she is destined to be a great leader. Many of us are convinced she has already established herself as one."

# HEARING DISABLED, NOT MENTALLY DISABLED

***For years, people have tried to tell Samuel Long, "You can't do that." But Sam never hears them.***

When Samuel Long was six months old, doctors told his parents, Pat and Darrell, that their son would be a severely handicapped, retarded child.

"We didn't totally believe them, because we never gave up hope," Pat says, "even though Sammy had 50 seizures a day. He'd go into a coma at the drop of a hat, with any infection. When he got chicken pox, he was out for 72 hours. He was in the hospital two to three times a month."

Doctors also told Sam's parents that he would never walk, but they didn't believe that, either. And at eighteen months, Sam learned to walk.

Something else important happened at around the same time. Another doctor discovered that Sam was not retarded, but deaf. He was *hearing* disabled, not *mentally* disabled.

Meanwhile, his parents noticed that Sam had a strong will and desire to learn. So they began to teach Sam to communicate, using facial expressions and gestures. They started teaching him sign language. Within six months, Sam had learned 100 words.

Doctors informed the family that Sam had a metabolic imbalance. His body didn't know how to use proteins. He also suffered from what they called a "white-matter degenerative brain disease." Part of the insulation at the base of his brain was stripping away.

**Samuel Long.** Photo courtesy of Darrell and Pat Long.

But Sam continued to amaze everyone with his progress. When he was four, his mother spent hours trying to teach him his colors. "What color, Sam?" she'd ask again and again. Communicating in sign language, she congratulated him each time he correctly named a color: a red rug, a brown chair, green trees. "Good boy, Sam," she motioned with her hands.

One afternoon, Sam had a surprise for her. The Longs

were in the process of painting their house, and Pat had gone inside to take a break, leaving Sam to play in the backyard. Suddenly he marched up to the back door, totally nude, his body covered with green house paint.

"What color, Mom?" he signed to his mother.

Her eyes stinging, she signed back, "Green."

Sam grinned. His hands flew with the retort, "Good girl, Mom!"

When Sam turned eight years old, he decided that he wanted to learn to breakdance. He read in the newspaper about a breakdancing class. When his mother called to ask if a deaf child could enroll, the instructor said, "No, he can't do that, because it will take too much time to teach him." Sam motioned, "Mom, let's pretend I'm not deaf. Sign me up anyway."

After the third lesson, the instructor pulled Sam's mother aside and said, "I don't want to alarm you, but I think your son might be a little hard of hearing. When I tell the kids to do something twice, Sam only does it once." Pat laughed and told the man that Sam was totally deaf.

The instructor was impressed with Sam's determination to learn. He let him stay in the class. "Next time, I'll hold up my fingers for Sam to tell him how many times to do something," the instructor promised. He even gave Sam chances to perform for audiences.

Next, Sam decided that he wanted to be a Boy Scout. And he wanted to be in a regular troop. Two turned him down, saying, "No, you can't do that; you'll have to join a handicapped troop." The family kept looking until they found a regular troop that would accept him. Sam's dad became his scoutmaster, and he's also Sam's best friend. In addition, Darrell Long is assistant scoutmaster for a handicapped troop, and Sam volunteers his time to help those scouts master their skills.

When it came time for Sam's troop to earn their swimming merit badges, Sam's doctor warned that he might never learn to swim. "He has too many muscle problems," the doctor said. But Sam wanted to earn his First Class rank, and swimming was a requirement. Even though the scout leaders offered to waive that requirement, Sam struggled long hours until he succeeded in learning the forward crawl and the backstroke. He also learned to dive, and he became quite a show-off, doing gainers—backward flips—off the board.

"I need a better education," Sam told his parents one day. "I'm twelve years old. Call the Missouri School for the Deaf."

Pat's mouth dropped open. Her heart fluttered. The Longs lived in Springfield, Missouri; the school for the deaf was in Fulton, 158 miles away. "Sam, you would have to stay there, live there," she said. "You could only come home on weekends and holidays. We'd hardly ever see you."

But Sam insisted that at the Missouri School for the Deaf, he wouldn't be limited to a "handicapped" curriculum. He wanted the chance to learn more.

His mother was sure that Sam would change his mind when he saw how far away the school really was. But when they arrived there, Sam surprised his parents once again. He didn't act nervous or frightened. He just turned to the principal and signed, "Where can I put my waterbed?"

"We were reluctant, but we let him go," Pat remembers. "And it has turned out great academically for him. He reads almost on grade level now. And he has friends. He plays football and basketball. It was harder for us than for him."

By the time Sam turned thirteen, he had outgrown his chronic sickness. He wanted to be more like other children. So when headphones became a craze, Sam got a set. He'd fit them over his ears, snap his fingers, and pretend he was listening to rhythmic beats.

One day, Sam and his mother were shopping at a local mall. Sam was wearing his headphones, and Pat was speaking to him in sign language. A sales clerk started writing a note to Pat, thinking *she* was deaf, not Sam. After all, what deaf kid would wear headphones? Sam laughed, enjoying the joke.

"Do you remember when I used to be handicapped?" he sometimes asks his mom. He is referring only to his years of sickness. Deafness is nothing to him.

During his thirteenth summer, Sam grew interested in helping other disabled young people. He spent the whole summer as a volunteer at the Springfield Park Board day camp for handicapped children. Although Sam insists he has no handicap himself, he believes that he knows how to communicate with and understand children with physical and mental problems.

He donated hundreds of hours to the day camp. He taught some children to canoe, watched over others at the waterfront, helped those with leg braces to walk, and hugged as many as he could. He patiently played catch with a child who consistently dropped the ball. He strutted along with his head held high and his shoulders thrust back, toting equipment, and laughing in his low, throaty voice.

His volunteer efforts spread to include the Special Olympics, an international athletic competition for disabled persons. He coached the Central High School girls' Special Olympics team, even though he was younger than the girls. His mom coached the boy's team.

They traveled to St. Louis, where the teams competed in the St. Louis District Tournament. Sam chaperoned Pat's boys in their room. He made sure that they were all out of bed in the morning and dressed in time for the games.

Sam coached his girls by drawing diagrams to point out what they could do to win. His team won first place. His mother's team only won third place, and Sam teased her mercilessly about it.

When Sam entered high school, he decided that he wanted to play football. The doctor at Children's Hospital at St. Louis looked at Sam's medical history and said, "No, you can't do that." But Sam argued that his health had improved. "This is my freshman year in high school," he said, "and I have dreamed about this for a long time."

The doctor chuckled at Sam's persistence, threw up his hands, and signed the permission form. Sam excelled in sports, traveling to five states in football and basketball tournaments.

In 1990, Sam received the "Spirit of Young American Award" from the Clairol Corporation for his volunteer work. He also received the "Yes, I Can" Award from the Foundation for Exceptional Children.

"He's quite an amazing boy," Pat says. "He's come a long way from being written off by doctors when he was a baby. It's getting to the point that I have to call and make appointments to see him. He does so much volunteer work. Everyone needs him. He's so busy. And happy. He has big plans now."

What are Sam's plans? When asked about them, he writes his answer:

> *I have a dream for my future. I will learn drafting. I will design and build houses. I want to make furniture for old people who do not have any money.... I do not want to use drugs. I want to be healthy and strong so I can work carrying heavy things into the house.... I want to buy a farm. I want to raise cattle, hogs, and horses. I love farm work.*
>
> *Once I had surgery on my leg. I was sick for one month. This was a challenge for me. I got better.*

*Once I told my dad, "Please quit using tobacco." It was a challenge for him, but he won.*

*Rick Sutcliff is a pitcher for the Chicago Cubs. I asked him how many games he's lost and won. He told me that his team won 23 and lost 16.... Rick Sutcliff makes his dreams come true. I can make my dreams come true, too.*

So don't ever tell Sam, "No, you can't do that." Sam will probably smile, but he won't hear you at all.

# REACHING OUT TO A STRANGER

*It was the middle of winter, and the woman had no shoes. Frank Daily looked down at his Nikes and made a decision.* Frank Daily stared down at the frozen ground. He kicked chunks of snow, blackened with car exhaust, to the side. He only pretended to listen to the chatter of his friends, Norm and Ed, as they all clambered aboard the Number 10 bus after school. He spouted out automatic answers to their questions: "Yeah, I aced the Milton test.... No, I can't tonight. I've got to hit the books."

Frank and his friends flopped down in the back of the Milwaukee city bus, along with several other high school boys, some from other schools. The bus belched a gray cloud out the back and headed west on Blue Mound Road.

Frank slouched into his seat. His hands hung from his two thumbs stuffed in the center of his belt. It had been another cold, gray day just a month ago in November when his world had come crashing down around him. He knew that his basketball skills were as good as the other boys'. His mom used to call him "the athlete of the season." When he was smaller, she had nicknamed him "Search and Destroy." He smiled at the memory.

The bus lurched away from a curb, and Frank instinctively braced his Nikes against the floor. "It must have been my size," he thought. "That had to be it. Five feet four. Since I'm new at Marquette High and only a freshman, the coach must have taken one look at me and decided I was too small to make the basketball team."

It wasn't easy starting a new school, especially an all-boys' Catholic school. The older boys tended to be a bit clannish. It was especially hard for Frank, because he had been a star athlete in all the sports in elementary school. Now, it seemed, he was a nothing.

Not only had he excelled in athletics before arriving at Marquette; he had also come alive to politics and history in the fifth and sixth grades. He recalled the advice his teacher, Don Anderson, had given him: "Look, Frank, if you'd put as much time into books as you do into basketball, you can do great in both."

"Well," Frank thought, "Anderson was right about the books, at least. My grades have been A's and B's ever since. Basketball is another story."

A loud horn and a screech of brakes somewhere behind the bus startled Frank. He looked at Norm and Ed. Norm was leaning his head against the window with half-shut eyes, his warm breath creating a circle of fog on the glass.

Frank rubbed his own eyes. He still remembered his stomach chilling into a frozen knot as he approached the locker room last month. He had read the team list posted on the locker room door, hoping, searching frantically for his name. It hadn't been there. It was missing.

No name. He had felt suddenly as if he had ceased to exist. Become invisible.

The bus jerked to a stop at the County Institutions grounds. The bus driver called to some noisy boys at the back to settle down. Frank glanced up at the driver, who had been dubbed "Kojak" by some of the guys on the bus because of his bald head.

A very pregnant woman hung onto the silver handrail and slowly pulled herself onto the bus. As she fell backward into the seat behind the bus driver, her feet kicked up, and Frank saw that she was in stocking feet.

As Kojak steered the bus back into traffic, he yelled over his shoulder, "Where are your shoes, lady? It ain't more than 10 degrees out there."

"I can't afford shoes," the woman answered. She pulled her fraying coat collar around her neck. Some of the boys at the back exchanged glances and smirked.

"I got on the bus just to get my feet warm," the woman continued. "If you don't mind, I'll just ride around with you for a bit."

Kojak scratched his bald head and shouted, "Now, just tell me how come you can't afford shoes?"

"I got eight kids. They all got shoes. There's not enough left for me. But it's okay, the Lord'll take care of me."

Frank looked down at his new Nike basketball shoes. His feet were warm and snug, always had been. And then he looked back at the woman. Her socks were ripped. Her coat, missing buttons, hung open around her stomach, as swollen as a basketball and covered by a smudgy dress.

Frank didn't hear anything around him after that. He wasn't aware of Norm or Ed. He just felt a warm thawing in his gut. The word "invisible" popped into his mind again. "An invisible person, marginal, forgotten by society, but for a different reason," he thought.

He would probably always be able to afford shoes. She probably never would. Under his seat, he pried the toe of one shoe into the heel of the other and slipped it off. Then the other shoe. He looked around. Nobody had noticed. He would have to walk three blocks in the snow. But the cold had never bothered him much.

Bus driver John Williams ("Kojak") and Frank Daily stand before the Number 10 bus. Photo by Jack Orton, Milwaukee Journal.

When the bus stopped at the end of the line, Frank waited until everyone else had emptied off. Then he reached under his seat and picked up his basketball shoes. He walked quickly up to the woman and handed them to her, looking down and saying, "Here, lady, you need these more than I do."

And then Frank hurried to the door and stepped down. He managed to land in a puddle. It didn't matter. He wasn't at all cold. He heard the woman exclaim, "See, they fit me just perfect!"

Then he heard Kojak call, "Hey, come back here, kid! What's your name?"

Frank turned around to face Kojak. At the same time, Norm and Ed asked where his shoes were.

Frank's cheeks burned. He looked in confusion at Kojak, his friends, and the woman. "Frank Daily," he said quietly. "My name is Frank Daily."

"Well, Frank," Kojak said, "I've never seen anything like that in the twenty years I've been driving this bus."

The woman was crying. "Thank you, young man," she said. She turned to Kojak. "See, I told you the Lord would take care of me."

Frank mumbled, "You're welcome." He smiled at the woman. "It's no big deal. Besides, it's Christmas."

He hurried off after Norm and Ed. It seemed to him that the grayness had lifted. On the way home, he hardly felt the cold beneath his feet at all.

• • • • •

*Frank Daily was 14 when this story took place. Although he didn't make the basketball team in his freshman year at Marquette High School, he did make the tennis team, which went on to win the state championship in his senior year.*

*When Frank was a freshman, he was 5'4"; today he's 6'2" and is studying Spanish and Politics at Wake Forest University in Winston-Salem, North Carolina.*

*Frank never saw the woman again. He is modest about what he did, and he doesn't consider it anything special. In his words: "We all have the potential to be heroic in some way."*

# HEROIC KIDS

"*A* hero is no braver than an ordinary man, but he is brave five minutes longer," Ralph Waldo Emerson once said. Humorist Will Rogers observed, "We can't all be heroes because somebody has to sit on the curb and clap as they go by."

You're about to meet six young people who were brave long enough to make a difference. Every one of them is worth clapping for.

What exactly is a "hero"? What kinds of people are heroes? When you think of a hero, do you picture a mythological character, like Hercules strangling a lion with his bare hands, or Atlas bearing the heavens on his shoulders? Do you think of someone with supernatural powers, such as Superman or a Ninja Turtle? Do you think of Rambo's muscles or Michael Jordan's slam-dunks? Or do you think of great leaders, like Dr. Martin Luther King, Jr., Geronimo, Mother Teresa, Gandhi, or Jesus?

Are heroes extra-intelligent? Extra-strong? Extra-brave? Larger than life? Although heroes may be some or all of these things, more often they're ordinary people. Sometimes they're quiet, sometimes they're boisterous. They are not necessarily smarter, stronger, or braver than anyone else.

In fact, the young heroes you're about to meet are people you probably would never notice in a crowd. If you saw one of them, you wouldn't jab your friend in the ribs, point, and whisper, "Oh, look. Here comes a hero." These heroes aren't always the leaders, and they almost never seek the limelight. If you ask them why they showed such courage, they'll all deny that they did. They'll say that they "just did what needed to be done."

You might even disagree with your friend over what a hero really is. You might feel that standing up for what you believe in is an act of heroism, especially when friends pressure you to do something you know is wrong. And you would *be right. You might feel that overcoming a personal fear is heroic, and you would be right again. To a painfully shy person, simply giving a speech in front of an audience might require heroic behavior.*

*There really isn't a single definition of heroism. But heroes do seem to have characteristics in common. For example, they usually care about other people. They usually have* empathy—*the ability to understand how others might feel. They behave in honorable ways that benefit others. Often, but not always, they are risk-takers. Frequently, they become role models, ideals for others to emulate and follow. Their behavior becomes a yardstick against which we measure ourselves.*

*Is a hero a hero all of the time? Occasionally, but more often an experience creates a "hero of the moment," someone who makes a brave choice at a difficult time. The heroes in this section are like that. These are not perfect kids. They are ordinary people who were thrown into difficult situations. But when faced with hard choices, they reached down inside themselves and found inner strength and courage that even surprised them. Some risked their own safety to help others. Some stayed brave a few minutes longer.*

*In other words, a hero can be anybody. If you look inside yourself, you might find a hero waiting. Maybe you won't discover that heroic you until a circumstance arises that requires a split-second action. You'll never know how far you can jump until a chasm appears in your path.*

*So who is a hero? Say hello to Ruben Ortega, who wrestled a rifle from a classmate. And Carl Boney and Michael Etowski, who saved a busload of children. And Andy D'Alesio, who rescued his friend from drowning. And Melinda Clark, who helped to save her brothers and sister in a fire. And Joshua Dennis, who was lost in a mine for five days. They're all just kids, but they're heroes, too. And any one of them might be* you.

# GUN CONTROL

**The student had a loaded gun and a room full of hostages. Police surrounded the school. Then Ruben Ortega got mad.**

Ruben Ortega wasn't thinking about being someone special on April 20, 1988. The day began like any other day. After pounding his alarm clock button, he stretched in bed. He was 18 years old and in his last year at San Gabriel High School.

An above-average student, getting mostly A's and B's, Ruben had never really been involved in school activities. Sometimes he wished he had been; sometimes he didn't care. But this morning, he felt a twinge of regret, like flipping on the TV only to catch the last five minutes of the Super Bowl.

He flopped his legs over the edge of his bed and ran his fingers through straight, brown hair. Then he stumbled over to the bathroom sink, splashed water on his face, and brushed his teeth. He didn't pause to eat breakfast.

Outside, the sun glistened from tiled roofs and splintered through palm tree branches into patches of yellow light. It was a typical California spring day—bright, but not hot—so Ruben grabbed his brown leather jacket as he dashed out the door. He hopped in his brother Amaury's Toyota 4x4.

Soon Ruben was walking through San Gabriel's swinging doors, probably for one of the last few times. His mother, Clodoalda, had divorced his father when Ruben was five years old. Although she worked as a secretary for a doctor, Ruben always knew that he had to help support himself. He and his brothers, Mario and Amaury, and sister, Leticia, had all learned to clean up after themselves, work hard, and stay out of trouble. But there hadn't been much time left over for school activities.

**Ruben Ortega.** Photo courtesy of Ruben Ortega.

Now that didn't matter. Soon it would be summer, and Ruben would be working full-time at Burrows and James Printing Shop. He loved the smell of ink and the hum of well-greased machines, magically cranking out posters, brochures, and labels. He planned to stay in the trade and work his way up.

The school day started off "pretty regular," Ruben remembers. "My first period was a metal shop class, where I was making a tool box. I went to second period, a psychology class. We discussed human behavior. Then there was chemistry. That was a real pain for me.

"Then I went to fourth period. It was a humanities class. We had two classes meeting together in a big class-room with the divider in the middle. It was always open. There were about 70 students in the class."

Normally, the class had two teachers, Julie Rivera and Kathleen Henderson. On that day, only one, Mrs. Rivera, was there. She asked the students to read a poem, "The Tables Turned," by William Wordsworth.

Ruben examined the poem, trying to decide what it should mean to him:

> *One impulse from a vernal wood*
> *May teach you more of man,*
> *Of moral evil and of good,*
> *Than all the sages can....*

About fifteen minutes into the class, a student named Jeff walked into the room with a rifle in one hand and a duffel bag in the other. No one seemed too concerned about the rifle, because everyone knew that Jeff was a practical joker. They all thought it was a toy.

Ruben says, "Jeff was well-liked and well-known. He had also been missing from school for a month. I had heard that he was having problems at home and was under some kind of therapy."

Carrying his rifle and bag, Jeff walked to the front of the class and started talking loudly about gun control. "We still thought he was joking around," Ruben says. "Ms. Rivera probably thought the rifle was a toy, because she sort of let him go on for a little bit. When it looked like he might be serious, she told him to put down the gun and sit down."

But Jeff kept talking, ignoring her. He said that if he wanted to, he could kill everyone in the class within seconds. Then he pointed the rifle at Ruben's friend,

Francisco, who was seated near the front of the class-room. Ruben's back stiffened against his wooden chair.

"Two other teachers, who were outside the room, saw him with the rifle and opened the door," Ruben con-tinues. "He told the teachers they were endangering the life of Francisco and to go back outside. The teachers closed the door."

Suddenly aware that Jeff wasn't kidding, four other students ran for the back door. Ruben explains, "Jeff pointed the gun away from my friend, shouted at the four to get away from the door, and fired a warning shot behind the last one that ran out.

"Once he fired the shot, all the students fell to the ground. Some girls started crying. Then Jeff told the teacher to leave. She refused. He yelled at her. We all told her to do what Jeff said. We knew he was mad, so we tried to talk her into leaving. We told her things might get worse if she stayed. She left the classroom."

Jeff called out the names of six or seven students in the class. "Barricade the doors," he ordered. So they emptied out two heavy, wooden bookshelves and slid them over the two doors. "I was terrified," Ruben says. "I was shaking and sweating.

"Jeff reached into the duffel bag he had brought in. He had a radio or walkie-talkie so he could talk to cam-pus security. He talked with someone and told them to back off. No one knocked on the door anymore, although the place was probably surrounded with police by then."

One frightened student asked Jeff, "Why are you doing this?" Jeff answered that he was advocating gun control. "You can't trust anyone to own a rifle, even if they seem honest," he said. "You can't trust everyone who buys a gun."

Then he asked the students if they were hungry. Everyone nodded. They didn't dare disagree. Jeff got on his walkie-talkie and ordered pizzas, demanding that they be there in ten minutes.

"Someone asked if he was really going to kill anyone," Ruben says. "He said he wouldn't if the police did what he said. If they didn't, he'd have to start killing people. He said he would shoot people he didn't know first.

"The phone rang. It was Ms. Henderson, the other teacher. She talked to Jeff, probably trying to tell him to give up. They had a good relationship. He ignored her. He said that if the pizzas weren't there in the next minute or so, there would be a dead body outside the door."

The students looked at one another, eyes wide, throats tight. Ruben sat in the back with his friends, trying to make a plan, whispering about how to stop him, jump him.

Suddenly, Ruben clenched his fists. He thought of his older brother, Mario. "He had been my father figure when I was young. I looked up to him a lot. He had a lot of things I wanted to have some day: a wife, a family, a nice house, car. Things like that."

Ruben knew he deserved to have those same things. So did everyone else in the room. Ruben felt the veins on his neck pulse as he watched each movement Jeff made.

"Jeff got comfortable," Ruben goes on. "He sort of sat down, leaning back on a chair with the gun between his legs. He had the phone in his left hand and his right hand on the barrel of the gun. Then I noticed that some other students were walking within five feet of him, and he didn't get mad.

"He wasn't looking at me. And I wondered if I could get close. I could go up to a student's desk that was about five feet from him, pretend it was my backpack on the desk, and that I wanted to get something from it.

"My heart was pounding. As I was walking, I watched Jeff out of the corner of my eye. I got to the desk.

I didn't even stop. I don't know how, but I just pounced beyond the desk and made a break for Jeff. He saw me as I grabbed the barrel of the rifle. He stood up, and we struggled together, shoving and yanking over the rifle."

Four other students jumped in. Together, they slammed Jeff against the wall and pinned him. Then they slid down the wall and fell onto the floor. Jeff still had the rifle.

"Then I got this idea," Ruben says. "I thought, 'What if the gun goes off again? Pointed at the class?' I still had my hand on the barrel, so I shoved it up toward the wall. Right as I did this, he fired the gun again. The bullet went above everyone's heads and lodged in the wall.

"We wrestled the rifle from him. One guy took it while two of us held him to the ground.

"When I looked up this time, I saw we were alone. While we were wrestling, all the other students knocked over the barricades and ran out. Then the police stormed in and took Jeff away."

Thirty-five minutes after Jeff had walked in, it was all over. The five students who had overpowered him slapped one another's backs and hugged. They left the room together to talk to the police.

As a result of the incident, Jeff was put under psychological observation and placed in a special program of incarceration and counseling. Meanwhile, Ruben became an instant hero at San Gabriel High. He received the California Governor's Award for his bravery. He and the four other students who had helped to wrestle Jeff to the ground were honored at graduation. And that's not all. In September, 1989, Ruben was awarded the Young American Medal for Bravery by President George Bush—in person.

Ruben may not have intended to be someone special, but he was. San Gabriel Mayor John D. Tapp put it this way: "As a result of Ruben Ortega's bravery and quick thinking, the potentially tragic incident was defused to the point that no injuries occurred, and there was no property damage to the school premises."

Was Ruben a hero? Does he fit the definition? His principal, Jack Mount, says, "I wouldn't have picked Ruben out in a crowd as a hero. But I think heroes are often like that. He is just a young man who was willing to do what his heart and gut told him to do."

# SAVING A BUSLOAD OF CHILDREN

*Something was wrong with the driver, and the bus was rushing toward trees. Could Carl Boney and Michael Etowski move fast enough?*

All day long in Fayetteville, North Carolina, it had been as hot and sticky as syrup. The air molecules seemed to move so slowly that nothing could possibly happen.

It was April 25, 1989, and Carl Boney and Michael Etowski, both fourteen, were riding the bus home from school. Although they attended different schools, they took the same bus; in fact, they had met there and become friends. The other 34 kids on the bus with them ranged in age from kindergarten through eighth grade.

Later, the two boys would talk about how they both had almost missed the bus that day. Carl was scheduled to stay after in detention for talking too much in class at St. Anne's Catholic School. He had also been caught drawing when he should have been reading. But he decided not to stay that night.

He'd make it up another time. Toting his books under one arm, he swung his feet up onto the bus.

"The driver, Richard Perry, said he felt hot and tired from a field trip he had just been on. I remember that," Carl says. "I took a seat at the back of the bus with the older guys."

At the same time, Mike was preparing to leave St. Patrick's Catholic School. As he opened his locker to gather his books, he and his friends shouted insults at one another. Locker doors banged shut, pounded by a dozen fists. The boys joked and threw wads of paper back and forth.

Soon summer would arrive in waves of heat and sweat. Mike told his friends that he would be a lifeguard for the Boy Scouts at Camp Durrant. Between that and working for his dad's construction business, his summer was mostly planned.

When Mike finally ran out the front door of St. Patrick's, the school bus was already crossing the parking lot. Mike shouted and waved his arm, chasing behind the bus, accidentally stumbling over his huge feet. At the edge of the lot, just before the bus turned onto the street, the driver saw Mike and stopped.

Mike teetered down the aisle as the bus took off. He plopped into a seat at the back next to his friend, Jennifer. Sensing the approach of a chocolate attack, he reached into his pack and pulled out a Snickers bar. Jennifer jabbed his ribs. "Hey, give that to me. I'm starving."

Mike waved the bar just out of her reach. "No way. This is my dinner."

Mike remembers, "I was going to split it with her, but when she tried to snatch it all, I had to tease her a little."

Jennifer leaned over Mike and grabbed his arm, biting in the air after the bar. Mike laughed and switched it to his other hand. Jennifer wrestled his arm down, and the heat-softened Snickers smooshed between their hands. Dividing up the spoils, they giggled and licked the chocolate from their fingers.

Meanwhile, Carl was talking to one of his friends. He told him that he was on his way to his mom's day-care center, where he would use the computer to run off her assignments for the next week. Carl loved fooling around with the computer.

The bus turned onto Rayford Road into busy rush-hour traffic. "A few minutes later, without any warning, I felt the bus weave to the right," Carl says. "I looked up and saw a utility pole ahead."

Mike felt the bus lurch, too. It happened so fast that no one had time to wonder. He turned away from Jennifer as the bus bounced up on the curb, then felt a jerking crash as it sheared past the utility pole and careened on down the road.

"I saw blue sparks and heard all this popping sound," Mike says. "I was slammed around. Then I jumped on the seat so I wouldn't get shocked. Everyone was freaking out. I looked up front. It didn't look like anyone was sitting in the driver's seat."

"I saw the bus was headed towards trees," Carl relates. Suddenly a memory flashed through Carl's mind: his brother, Larry, teaching him to drive a few months before. "I jumped up and ran to the front of the bus. And then I saw the driver was leaning to one side of his seat."

Without taking time to think, Carl struggled over the driver's body and forced his own foot down, shoving Perry's leg to one side. He stretched out the whole length of his five feet, two inches and jammed his foot on the brake. At the same instant, he grabbed the wheel and barely steered the bus away from the trees looming ahead.

But because Perry's foot was pressed heavily against the gas pedal, as Carl let up on the brake, the bus lunged forward again. Carl wrestled the steering wheel and steered the bus toward the stoplight.

Mike reached the front of the bus at this moment. He helped Carl to steer as Carl pressed on the brake a second time. Mike flipped the ignition off, and the bus slammed to a halt.

Children screamed, cried, and banged into each other. Mike shouted at the older kids to help the little ones off the back of the bus next to a grassy yard at the side of the road. Carl helped the children down. Some of the children sobbed; some laughed hysterically and then cried.

Mike continues, "I turned around and looked at the bus driver. I shook him, and I saw he had a lump on his head. I thought he had probably passed out and then hit his head.

"There was a large man looking in the bus window. I shouted at him to help me get Mr. Perry off the bus. Together we dragged him outside and stretched him out in the grass."

Calling on his Boy Scout training, Mike treated the driver for shock. "I raised his feet and loosened his shirt. He was hot, then cold and clammy. He wasn't breathing, but I felt a slight pulse. So I opened his airway and kept it open until the medics from Fort Bragg came.

"There were two nurses, a man and a woman. They put a neck brace on him. I don't know why they did that. I kept saying, 'Give him CPR,' while I kept him breathing. He was periodically coughing. They checked his heart rate and blood pressure.

"About then, the paramedics arrived, and they told me to beat it. They put electrodes on him and rushed him to the hospital."

As Mike stumbled onto the grass, friends pounced on him and Carl, smothering them with thanks and bear hugs. Only then did Mike begin to realize what had happened. He looked around. None of the children had been injured.

It turned out that Richard Perry had suffered a stroke while driving the bus. Sadly, he never recovered. He died later in the hospital.

The day after Carl and Mike saved the bus and the children, their story was in all the newspapers. Many called the two boys heroes. Their classmates stared at them and whispered. And although the parents of the children who were on that bus would certainly agree that the boys are heroes, both Carl and Mike deny it. "We're just ordinary boys," Mike says. "What we did was natural," Carl adds. In their own minds, they just did what needed to be done.

Mike (L) is now 6'2" tall. He plays football for his high-school team. Carl has grown into a slim young man almost 6' tall. He plans to play football next year. Both boys plan to go to college. Photo courtesy of Cramer Gallimore.

# COURAGE IN A FIRE

**The house was filled with smoke and flames. And Melinda Clark couldn't find her little brother.**

Melinda Clark pulled the blanket up under Courtney's chin and whispered, "Good night, Corky." It was 10:00 p.m. and time for bed. Melinda grinned and patted the huge lump under the covers created by Courtney's three-foot panda. The two sisters shared the same room, but thirteen-year-old Melinda didn't mind at all. Courtney, who was only four, seemed like her baby, too.

Melinda jumped under her own covers, but she didn't pull them up. Even though it was February and there was snow frozen on the ground outside, it seemed unusually warm that night, especially for Everett, Pennsylvania.

Something wet slopped along her cheek. "Oh, Beau. You're a good dog." The miniature collie licked her again. His tail thumped alongside her bed as she rubbed his sable fur.

Melinda's nose twitched at the smoky odor in the air. It was probably just the wood stove downstairs. Fumes traveled up the staircase easily. Melinda shut her eyes.

Two-year-old Justin startled her as he burst through the doorway. He ran over to Melinda's bed and banged his fists on her. "Mom hurt!" His face flushed red.

"What?" Melinda jumped up. The carpet felt very warm as she dropped her bare feet onto the floor. The smoky smell was stronger as she stood up.

What was going on? She rubbed her tingling cheeks and ran into the hall between the two second-story bedrooms. She paused. As she opened the door at the top of the stairs, smoke sucked up the steps in swirls. Orange flames crackled and leaped toward her like snatching fingers. She covered her hot face and screamed.

**Melinda Clark.** Photo courtesy of Mr. and Mrs. Terry Clark.

"Wayne!" She turned and yelled for her twelve-year-old brother. Although his bedroom light was on, she couldn't even see his bed through the ballooning smoke. But Wayne fought through the gray haze and stumbled into her. He was in his underwear.

"My window!" Melinda yelled.

Together they ran into Melinda's room to the double windows, where Wayne began struggling with the stubborn latch on the chest-high ledge.

"Pull! Shove it!"

"I'm yanking!"

The fiberglass curtains melted down the sides of the window.  Flecks of hot plastic burned into Wayne's bare back.

Melinda smashed her fist against the latch.  *If they couldn't get it open, they were going to die....*

Wayne banged at the latch, too.

Suddenly it budged, then slipped open.  But as they shoved on the window, it held tightly shut, swollen from the waves of heat.

Courtney yanked on Melinda's pink nightgown, screaming and crying.  She coughed and choked in the acrid fumes.

Melinda's eyes stung.  She gritted her teeth.  They weren't going to die in these flames!  "Shove, Wayne!  Together!  Now!"  They banged on the window.  "Again!  Harder!"  She coughed.  She threw all her hundred pounds behind the thrust.

Wayne shoved, too, and together they finally forced the stubborn window open.

Melinda told Wayne to climb out on the plastic porch roof.  She handed Courtney over the window.  Then Melinda pulled herself over the window ledge.

The three children walked to the edge of the roof, looking for a way down.  Wayne jumped to the ground to catch the younger kids.

Suddenly Melinda looked at Wayne, her eyes round circles "Justin!  Where's Justin?  *Justin!*"  She screamed.  He had been right with them!

Without pausing for a breath, she turned around and climbed back over the hot window ledge.

"Justin!" she called.

She dropped onto her hands and knees and crawled low on the hot carpet. She found the closet and felt her hands around. No Justin. She tried to call, but she choked. Her throat felt like hot coals. Yanking on the tangled nightie under her burning knees, she bumped into Courtney's five-foot tall toy dog and duck, knocking them both over.

Could Justin have gone back into his bedroom? If he had, she'd never make it through the smoke and flames, which now sucked up the open staircase and window as if a vacuum were outside the window.

Stretching out flat, she felt under Courtney's bed. No Justin.

She coughed in spasms and grabbed at her throat. She couldn't breathe. She wasn't going to make it.

As she crawled toward the window, she heard a noise. Her bed. Was that where the noise came from? She scrambled across the floor and reached under her bed, her hand bumping into fur. Beau. He whimpered again and licked her hand. She searched her fingers past Beau and touched hair. Justin. He was there hiding, too. "Thanks for whimpering, Beau," she thought.

She grabbed Justin by his hair and pulled him out from under the bed. He clung to her like a baby Koala as she crawled back toward the window.

She lifted him over the window ledge and climbed out behind, gasping for mouthfuls of air. But as she stepped onto the plastic roof, her foot crashed through melting plastic up to her knee. She ripped her leg out of the hole and moved to the edge of the roof.

A second later, the picture window below them exploded. Shattering glass flew out thirty feet.

Courtney and Justin screamed and pulled at Melinda's arms.

"Beau!" Melinda yelled. She looked behind at the flames licking out the bedroom window. "Oh, Beau!" She tried to swallow, and without another pause, she pushed both younger children off the roof into the snow eighteen feet below. She leaped behind them, practically smashing Justin as she hit the ground.

A trooper who had seen the fire from the road scooped up the children and carried them across the glass and snow to his car.

"Mommy!" Justin cried.

"Where's Mom?" Melinda asked. She ran up to the neighbor's porch looking for her mom, just as Mrs. Clark ran across the snow to wrap Melinda in her arms. "I was calling 911," she choked, as she grabbed Wayne in a hug. "I was down the basement changing the wash. I saw you at the top of the stairs. I yelled at you to get out."

The trooper carried the little ones into the neighbor's house. They called Mr. Clark, who was working the night shift at Everite Door Manufacturing.

Melinda dropped onto a beanbag chair. The voices and faces swirled around her. She passed out for a few moments.

When she came to, she was in an ambulance. The red light flashed. The siren screamed. She drifted in and out of consciousness several more times before reaching the hospital.

Melinda was treated for smoke inhalation, as were her brothers and sister. Melinda's nightgown was melted in spots and although it stuck to her skin, her body beneath it wasn't burned.

Both she and Wayne suffered minor burns, however. Melinda's leg was scratched and burned from where it had broken through the roof, while Wayne's back was burned in small spots from the fiberglass curtains. Courtney and Justin received scratches in their tumble from the overhang.  Their pajamas were scorched.  But all four children were alive.

Justin kept repeating, "An angel picked me up and threw me out the window.  It was a real angel.  I know it."

Melinda smiled.  She hugged Justin and closed her eyes.

No one could determine the cause of the fire.

"It wasn't until the next day when we went back that I got really scared," Melinda remembers.  "When we walked into the downstairs, it was really strange.  Some things were burned, and other things weren't.  Like, the fish was still alive, swimming in his bowl in the dining room.  But our bedrooms were ruined."

Her brown eyes suddenly fill with tears.  "Beau didn't make it."  She looks down.  "I had to leave him under my bed."

But Justin did make it, because Melinda, the small angel, crawled back into the flames to save her brother.  Her fast action and courage wouldn't let her give up.

# RESCUING A FRIEND FROM DROWNING

*The boys fell into the icy water. Heavy, wet winter coats dragged them down. Then Andy D'Alesio saved the life of his friend.*

Nine-year-old Andy D'Alesio hustled into his mom's Chrysler mini-van.

"Slide over, Andy," his mother demanded. "Make room for Valerie. And hurry up!" She swore at his slowness and lack of concern. "We'll be late for your basketball game."

Rebecca D'Alesio revved up the engine and blew into her hands. It was an icy Saturday morning in Reynoldsburg, Ohio. The last few days in February had been cold enough to freeze the grass into a crunchy crust.

Andy slid over the upholstered cushion to make room for Valerie. He didn't argue about sharing the seat with his little sister. She was only six years old, and he often protected her. Now, if it had

been his twelve-year-old brother, Dave, Andy probably
wouldn't have budged. So he must have been glad it was
Valerie, because he didn't want to be late for his game,
either. He did scold his mom for swearing, however.

Soon Andy was zooming around the basketball
court. He didn't complain when the referee called a foul
on him. Good sportsmanship was important to him.
Self-confident and solidly built, he dribbled the ball
quickly around the guards to score 16 points for his winning team.

After the game, Andy asked if he could go to
Michael's house to play. His mother laughed. "Aren't
you too tired? What if I say no?" she joked.

Andy started arguing. "How do you know how tired
I feel? That's not fair! But this time, I'll wear a coat,"
he bargained.

"Whoa! Slow down!" Rebecca said, tugging on the
long hairs at the nape of his neck. She remembered their
argument from the day before, when Andy had refused
to wear even a sweatshirt to school. She didn't want
another disagreement. "I'm only teasing," she laughed.
"You can go. You know you're my favorite middle child."

Andy groaned at their familiar joke. "Not again!
I'm your *only* middle child," he grinned.

She swatted his bottom playfully. "Beat it," she said.

Andy grabbed his coat from his closet and banged
the door behind him.

Standing at Andy's bedroom window, Rebecca
pulled the plaid curtains aside and peered down at her
son. She smiled as she watched him force his basketball
into a plastic sack and hook it over the handlebars of his
dirt bike. His blond hair spiked up on top, like a
rooster's comb.

And, like a rooster, Andy wasn't afraid to speak up.
Rebecca realized that he was the hardest of her children

to live with. He was the outspoken one, emotionally intense. He'd tell her he hated her one minute, then apologize and hug her the next. She thought it ironic that he never challenged authority at school.

"I remember watching him as he rode off," she says. "I hoped that he would be careful on his bike. He was always so darned sure of himself."

She turned from the window and looked around his cluttered bedroom. The walls were plastered with posters of sports heroes, like Bernie Kosar, star quarter-back of the Cleveland Browns, and Michael Jordan of the Chicago Bulls. She shook her head at the unmade bed sheets dragging onto the floor and the baseball cards scattered across the carpet. There was only one peaceful solution. She walked out and closed his bedroom door behind her.

Andy's mom had to take Valerie to an all-day Girl Scout International Festival, so the two of them got ready to leave. Andy's brother, Dave, was plopped in front of the TV playing Nintendo. Rebecca knew that her husband, Michael, would soon be returning from the Georgia Pacific Lumber Company, where he worked as a sales manager. She wasn't worried about Andy's coming home to an empty house.

Later, when Andy returned, he brought Mike with him. Michael D'Alesio smiled to see the two boys. Before Andy was even in the door, he was asking his father, "Would you please drive Mike and me to the TCBY Yogurt place? His mom took us last time. And it's only fair that you take us. And I owe a yogurt to Mike. His mom bought them last time...please. We should always share, shouldn't we?"

Andy's dad laughed. "Go on, get in the car," he said. On the way to the frozen yogurt shop—where the two boys would order their favorite, vanilla yogurt with Reese's Pieces—Andy and Mike wrestled and joked.

A few days earlier, Mike had helped Andy to make a felt banner for his First Sacrament of Reconciliation (confession), an important event for Catholic young people. It would be a big moment for Andy, but now he laughed and told his friend that CCD—which they both knew stood for "Confraternity of Christian Doctrine"—really meant "Cool Catholic Dudes."

"Let us walk home, Dad," Andy pleaded as they pulled up in front of the yogurt shop. "I know the way." His dad knew that his confident son could easily find his way home. Both boys were dressed warmly; Andy had on a long-sleeved jersey and a coat, and Mike was wearing his winter coat. So Mr. D'Alesio dropped them off, warned them not to take too long, and returned home.

**Andrew D'Alesio.** Photo courtesy of Rebecca and Michael D'Alesio.

The boys must have giggled, jabbing each other in the ribs, as they sauntered down the sidewalk after finishing their yogurts. They had been close friends for three years. They admired each other's athletic abilities. Mike was a much smaller, less husky boy than Andy; he played soccer and wrestled.

Andy's mother, Rebecca, relates, "The boys took a

shortcut through a housing development where there was a pond encircled by several houses. Because it had been so cold the last few days, the pond had frozen on top."

She swallows before going on. "Andy and Mike must have played on it, sliding across, knowing the ice was thin, but probably believing the water was not very deep."

Mike would later tell Andy's parents the details.

As the boys scooted across the thin, frozen layer of ice, it suddenly cracked, then split into pieces. Both boys fell through into the sub-zero water. They thrashed around, reaching out their arms to grab something, anything, trying to keep their faces above the surface of the water. It was several inches deeper than they were tall. Heavy, wet coats dragged at their bodies. Each time they tried to pull themselves up, a chunk of ice broke off in their hands.

"Andy must have known one of them had to get out," his mother says. She pauses, clears her throat. "He knew how to take charge. Andy dived down under the water, grabbed Mike by the ankles, and shoved him up onto the ice. He shouted at Mike to go get help."

Mike struggled to the top of the bank and wandered through the neighborhood, wet and dazed. A man who was walking his dogs saw Mike hunched over, shivering and incoherent. The man took him into his home and warmed him. After Mike stopped shaking and could talk, the man asked him what had happened. He heard Mike's story and immediately called 911.

By the time the rescue squad arrived at the scene, Andy had been submerged for almost thirty minutes. The men stomped holes in the ice with their boots and searched under the water twenty-five feet from shore. Finding the unconscious boy, they pulled him from the water with poles.

They rushed Andy to the Children's Hospital in Columbus, where doctors struggled frantically to restore his vital signs. Finally they dropped their hands to their sides, throwing down their instruments. They were unable to revive the courageous little boy who had saved his friend but could not save himself. Andrew William D'Alesio died on February 25, 1989.

It shocked the neighborhood. Andy's family mourned. Everyone mourned. Flowers and letters poured into the D'Alesio home.

In remembrance of Andy, the principal and teachers at Rosehill Elementary created a plaque with Andy's picture, which hangs in the front hall of the school. Each year, the school chooses two fourth-graders to receive an Athletic and Good Sportsmanship Award at a special assembly. The two students who most exemplify Andy's good sportsmanship are further honored by having their names engraved on the plaque beneath his picture.

Several friends and neighbors passed a petition asking the mayor to do something special in Andy's memory. So Reynoldsburg Mayor Bob McPherson dedicated a ball field at Kennedy Park to Andy. The plaque reads: "This field is dedicated to the memory of Andy D'Alesio who on February 25, 1989, gave of his own life so that another could live. In the memory of Andy D'Alesio will the youth of Reynoldsburg continue to grow."

In November, 1990, the U.S. Department of Justice awarded Andy the Young American Medal for Bravery. But an even greater tribute came from Mike's mother, who said, "If there had been any boy other than Andy in the pond with Mike, two boys would have died."

Andy's physical education teacher, Jerry Miller, sums it up: "Andy was the ultimate team player....In our hearts, we know he has made the Big League."

# FIVE DAYS
# IN A MINE

*His dad thought he was with the older boys. They thought he was with his dad. But Joshua Dennis was alone in the dark, deep underground, with nothing but his faith.*

On a Friday evening in September, 1989, Joshua Dennis accompanied his father on a Boy Scout trip to explore Hidden Treasure Mine in Stockton, Utah.

Stockton was an old mining ghost town that had flourished off and on from 1865 to 1956. The mine had become a favorite place for scouts, who regularly tromped through the tunnels and investigated the abandoned ore stopes, the step-like excavations where ore is mined. A sign at the entrance said "No Trespassing," but the seal at the opening had long ago been eroded away by wind and water.

Since Joshua was only ten years old and a Cub Scout, he watched as the older boys pitched tents between tall pine trees outside the entrance to the mine. While they worked, one of the scout leaders sketched out the history of the mine. It was once a good source of silver and lead, he told them; Indians had discovered it long ago. Then soldiers and

117

private fortune-seekers had picked at the walls until the mine was taken over by the U.S. Smelting and Mining Company in 1950.

Josh listened for a while, then joined in a wild game of Capture the Flag.

When his father, Terry Dennis, called him away from the game, Josh followed him and three other scouts into the mine. A larger group had gone in a few minutes earlier. The plan was to catch up with them inside.

The three-foot-high mine entrance was on a hill covered with sage and rabbit brush. Josh entered feet-first and slid down into a tunnel. Other scouts had told him that sometimes there were bats or rats at the beginning of the mine, but Josh didn't see or hear anything suspicious. The ground was damp and slippery near the opening from a recent rain shower.

"I'm glad you always take me on scout trips with you," Josh told his dad. Terry squeezed his son's shoulder.

Josh shined his flashlight around the tunnel. It looked about seven feet tall and five feet wide. The walls glistened from conglomerates of silver, lead, rock, and a damp shininess. He stumbled over a railroad tie and abandoned railroad tracks, where wooden carts had once transported hand-picked silver ore treasure.

He could imagine the sound of the miners' noisy chatter, could almost see them stomping along in heavy boots and hard hats, sweat and dirt smeared over their muscular arms, crusted in the folds of their fingers and under their nails.

His dad interrupted his daydreaming. "Let me take the flashlight, Josh, so I can light the path for all of us." They hurried along the trail behind the scouts who had gone before.

Suddenly one of the other three scouts in Josh's group cried out, "I can't see anything! I can't see even

with the light.  I'm night blind.  Get me out of here!"
Terry could hear that the scout was close to panic.  He
reached for the boy's arm and said, "Don't be scared.  I'll
take you out."

Terry assumed that Josh would continue following
the two older scouts.  He took the frightened scout back
to the opening of the mine.

It wasn't until about 9:30 p.m., when the other
scouts climbed out of the mine, that Terry realized Josh
was not among them.

"I thought Josh was with you," he said.

"But we thought he was with *you*," they replied.

Quickly gathering a small search party, Terry
scrambled back into the mine.  They flashed their lights
around and called Josh's name.  With a sick feeling in his
stomach, Terry remembered that some of the older
scouts had been teasing Josh because he was only a
"cub."  They had hidden behind crevices in the mine,
turning off their lights and jumping out at him.

He imagined his young son, wandering in the black-
ness of the cave with no light.

By 2:30 a.m., the scout leaders contacted the local
sheriff.  It was early Saturday morning, September 23,
1989, and the big search for Joshua Dennis had begun.

The Tooele County Search and Rescue Team arrived,
along with the Salt Lake Search and Rescue Team.  Each
team that went into the mine attached colored ribbons to
any walls and outcrops they passed.  This told other
groups that those areas had already been investigated,
saving precious time.

Soon the human rescue teams were joined by the
American Search Dogs, who are specially trained to find
lost people.  They were given Josh's pillow to sniff.
Outside the mine, the dogs picked up Josh's scent near
two shafts—one with deep pools of water, the other with

poisonous gases inside. But Josh had been seen walking near the holes before entering the mine. That must be why the dogs had picked up his scent there, the searchers agreed.

Some of the dogs were taken inside the mine on leashes. Because there was no ventilation to carry his scent, the dogs couldn't help find Josh.

By now Josh's mother, Janeen, had arrived from their home in Salt Lake City. She and Terry would stay at a hotel near the mine to be close to Josh. Pacing in her hotel room, Janeen remembered that a week before, while waiting at a stop light, she had had a premonition. A strange feeling had made her spine tingle. She had imagined that her family would soon face a difficult problem, and that it would involve Joshua. She had shaken her head, told herself not to think morbid thoughts, and shoved the strange feeling from her mind. Now it returned.

She also remembered something else. A few weeks earlier, when Josh had been in charge of their family night together (a tradition in the Mormon church), their discussion had been on the topic of faith. She could almost hear Josh's innocent voice: "If you have faith, you can do anything."

"Well, almost anything," Janeen had corrected him.

"No, Mom," Josh had disagreed. "You can do *anything*."

Janeen rubbed the goose bumps on her arms. She prayed that her son would keep that faith now.

Utah Power and Light sent in a rescue team. Over 200 volunteers combed the mine and the surrounding hills. Many members of the Dennis family's church entered the search. One neighbor, Jess Garcia, paid his construction crew to join the search and bought everyone boots to wear. They explored 21 miles of tunnels, a labyrinth on six different levels. They found more than

100 air shafts and tunnels, many with sudden drops straight down.

Although colored ribbons soon decorated every turn in the mine, there was still no sign of Josh. Searchers began to doubt that he was in the mine at all. Maybe he was lost in the hills between Ophir and Dry Canyons. No one knew.

The sheriff's dispatcher told Terry and Janeen, "We've searched every inch three times, and he's not there."

If Josh were still inside, officials concluded, he was probably buried in a rockslide. But they were 85 to 90 percent sure that he was no longer inside the mine. They moved their search to the outside.

But family members kept urging, "Don't give up. He's still in the mine. We know it."

Josh's mom told the searchers, "I keep having impressions that Josh has climbed, that he is high up." The searchers insisted that Josh wouldn't have been able to see well enough to climb up anywhere.

A couple of old miners joined the search, turning up no new clues. Sunday dawned. Television and newspaper reporters following the story asked, "How long can a small boy survive without food or water? Up to three days without water, longer without food." A whole city silently prayed that Joshua would be found before it was too late.

A mine historian, John Skinner, heard about the lost boy when he returned home from a vacation in Montana. John knew Hidden Treasure Mine like the back of his hand. And, like Josh, he had been only ten years old when he went inside it for the first time. He could remember feeling small and frightened by the total darkness, the complete lack of sound, the utter stillness.

John's father, grandfather, and great-grandfather had all worked in the mine. John had developed an interest in the mine's history and was writing a book about mines. He had explored Hidden Treasure some 110 times and knew each crevice and bend. He realized that he was the best person to try to find Joshua.

"I drove down and attempted on Sunday to go in," John relates. "The search teams there said they didn't need me. There was a roadblock in the way at Soldier Canyon.

"I knew that Buckhorn Mine was connected to Hidden Treasure. So I hiked up Ophir Canyon and went into Buckhorn, but it was too unsafe. It was in bad condition. I hiked back down the canyon. The search team told me again that they didn't need my help, that there were already enough people.

"I didn't sleep very well Sunday night," John remembers. "I dreamed about places in the mine where Josh might be. I kept waking my wife up. Somehow I knew it was up to me to find the boy."

John tried to reach the mine again on Monday, but the sheriff stopped him. John was growing increasingly frustrated. He knew he could help, but no one wanted him. On Tuesday, he stayed away.

But John knew that Josh was still alive. Call it instinct, or inspiration; *something* told him. And he couldn't just give up.

"On Wednesday, I got smart," he says. "I avoided the roadblock and went up a back way."

He stopped at Penny's Diner. While munching a cheeseburger, he drew a map on a paper napkin, scribbling X's on the places where he thought the boy might be.

"But when I left the diner and reached the mine, a deputy stopped me. By this time, they thought Josh must be outside of the mine. I talked hard to the deputy and persuaded him to let me through. Then I went to the sheriff and showed him my map. They had tried everything else, so they finally let me in the mine."

John led a group of eighteen searchers back into the mine. "There were three different sections where I thought Josh might be," he recalls. "One was a spot where the timber had knocked a hole in the path. I thought he might have slipped through it. But we didn't find him there. And we didn't find him in the second spot.

"The third and last place I checked was around a drift to the stope area. There were colored ribbons hanging everywhere. Lots of people had already been there, maybe ten teams. By this time, there were only two guys with me—Ray Guyman and Gary Christensen, both from Utah Power and Light. We had separated from the others.

"About twenty-five minutes after we had entered the mine, I shined my light upward and asked, 'Have you searched up there?'"

And that's when Ray Guyman first heard a sound. Was it the wind? A pebble falling? Or a piece of tin on the trail? He held up his hand for the others to stop talking. "I think I hear something," he said. The others looked at him funny. Everyone knew that Ray was very hard of hearing.

John listened. Then he heard it, too. He shouted, "Keep yelling!" and listened again. This time, all three men heard the small voice crying for help.

John and the other men scrambled toward the direction of the call. John's heart skipped. Could it be Josh? Could he still be alive and able to call out?

Gary was the first one up the slope. He caught some blondish hair in the beam of his flashlight and scrambled toward it like a mountain goat. Josh slid down the slope on his bottom, right into Gary's arms.

"We all wrapped around him and hugged him," John remembers. "We stood there and cried like babies. How could the little guy still be alive after five days? He had

had no water, no light, no food, no company. It was a mystery.

"It looked like Josh had crawled up the steep hill into an ore stope about 500 feet above where he had separated from his dad," John explains. "He had obviously gone though a hole about 150 feet back up the hill and reached a dead end in an old ore pocket. He was on a ledge about 25 feet back and six feet wide. You couldn't even see the hole unless you stepped right below it. It was hidden by rocks and debris. Searchers must have come within twenty-five feet of him without seeing him. Josh could have been asleep, but sound doesn't travel well in that mine. If the three of us hadn't separated from the others, we might not have heard his cry over the shoe thuds."

Josh didn't cry when John and the others found him. His eyes were wide open. He was very weak, but he acted calm, as though he had been expecting them. He said he knew his dad was outside. And he had no idea he had been in the cave for five whole days.

As the men carried him triumphantly out of the mine, Josh squinted his eyes painfully in the bright light. Cameras flashed in his face. He couldn't believe the fuss people were making over him.

Josh was rushed to Tooele Hospital and then transferred to Primary Children's Hospital in Salt Lake City. He was treated for dehydration and frostbite on his blackening feet. At first, doctors thought they might have to amputate some toes, but his feet slowly recovered.

Josh was in a wheelchair for a couple of weeks until he was able to walk again. Dr. Ted Jenkins said that by staying in one place and sleeping a lot, Josh had slowed down his metabolism. This had saved his body fluids, and probably his life.

"His feet hurt him badly for the next while, and he would wake up crying," Janeen says. "It also took him a few months before he could skateboard again. But he's never had any nightmares from the experience."

Parents, friends, and reporters asked Josh how he managed to stay alive in the mine. And Josh shared his adventure.

"After my dad left, I followed the two other scouts. But they started walking faster and faster, probably to catch up with their friends ahead of them. I tripped over rocks to try to keep up with them. I guess they thought I went out with my dad."

With no flashlight, he had to keep the older boys' shadowy forms in sight. He had gone about 2,000 feet into the cave when he became separated from them. "They turned a corner, and I couldn't see any light anymore. I lost them. I really wasn't scared, because I thought my dad would come back. I started to walk back, and I prayed that I could find my way out. It was pitch black. I couldn't even see my hand if I put it in front of my face.

"I thought I could find my way out at first. I followed with my hand on the right side along the wall. I didn't know, but the left side was the correct way. So I took a wrong turn.

"I stumbled over some rocks, and I almost fell down a steep place. I thought I'd better climb up and try to find a way out. I followed some railroad tracks, and then they stopped. I found a tunnel of some kind. It was warmer. My sneakers and socks were wet. There were puddles. I started wishing I had a flashlight. And then I bumped my head. I climbed on my hands and knees up a steep hill to a ledge."

Then Josh remembered what his parents had told him to do if he ever got lost: "Stay still and wait for someone to find you, and try not to get scared." Besides, he wasn't the first kid in his family to get lost. Two years earlier, when his little sister, Terra, was only three, she had wandered away from the family cabin. She later said that an angel brought her back. His other sister, Danielle, got lost at Disneyland. Josh prayed for her, and she was found. Then his little brother, Jacob, disappeared at the Twenty-Fourth of July Pioneer Parade a few months before. His family found him, too.

And Josh knew that someone, sooner or later, would find him. "I prayed a lot to be found," he says.

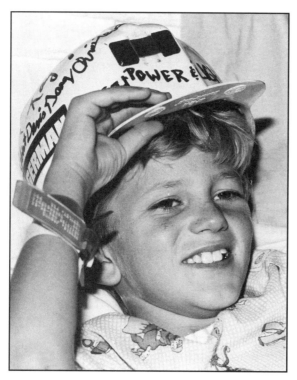

Joshua Dennis wearing the hard hat autographed by his rescuers.

He curled up on the ledge, wrapped his coat around him, and waited. Underneath, he was wearing only a T-shirt, jeans, and tennis shoes. He wasn't too cold, except for his throbbing feet. When they grew numb, they stopped hurting.

"Sometimes I sang songs, like 'I Am a Child of God' and 'Everybody's Got to Have a Hero.' I knew that whoever found me would be my hero.

"I slept a lot. It really only seemed like a day or two. I woke up once and was hungry. Then I remembered I had a pack of Licorice Nibs in my pocket, so I ate a few pieces a little bit at a time, and then I was so hungry that I gobbled the rest."

Josh dreamed a lot about pizzas and hamburgers. Once he dreamed that he was eating a French fry with ketchup. When he woke up, he found that he was trying to eat a little rock with mud on it.

"Once in a while, I heard voices and shoe thuds, but they didn't hear me when I called. They seemed far away, like in a dream.

"I cried just once," he says in a quiet voice. "And I prayed a lot for courage, and I felt comforted. I felt that I wasn't alone."

His Mom and Dad had told him stories about how the Father in Heaven and his angels would protect him. Josh thought about those stories. "I didn't get lonely or scared after that. I knew someone was taking care of me."

Josh is modest about his ordeal. When he arrived home from the hospital and found his house and the whole neighborhood decorated with yellow ribbons, he wondered again why everyone was making such a big deal out of it. Four hundred neighbors waited for him with a surprise party. Hundreds of yellow balloons were released and floated into the sky. Josh received over 1,000 letters of congratulations from friends and strangers, including President George Bush.

Did the experience and all the attention change Josh? Well, he still plays basketball and football, collects sports cards, and loves scouting.

But his mother thinks he has changed. "He's more responsible," she smiles. "He does his homework. He even keeps his room clean now. And he reads the scriptures every night. He read the *New Testament* in about two months. Now he's trying to finish the *Book of Mormon*. He wants to be a missionary when he turns nineteen, and then become a policeman.

"Something happened to him in that mine. He stayed alive somehow, and he grew up a lot."

John Skinner, the man who found Josh after other searchers told him he "wasn't needed," thinks he knows how Josh survived. "The thing that saved Joshua for five days when he was without water, food, and light, or even companionship, was his courageous faith. That was Joshua's secret."

John wipes his eyes. "They've taken a lot of money and wealth out of Hidden Treasure Mine over the years. But the greatest treasure ever found there was a small, alive, ten-year-old boy with incredible faith."

# KIDS SAVING THE ENVIRONMENT

*W*hat kind of place will the Earth be in 2050? Will several species of turtles, wildfowl, and insects be extinct? Will tropical rain forests continue to topple under bulldozers? Will acid rain deface more historic monuments? Will our garbage pile up in huge pyramids of waste, polluting land and water?

Or will all people join in worldwide action to save our planet? Lots of kids are working to improve the world. They know that in this age of disposable diapers, cups, and batteries, all of us must ask ourselves, "Is our Earth also disposable?" But it isn't too late. And kids like you can make the difference.

You're about to read about several kids who have tackled problems in the environment with courage, creativity, and commitment. Like the students at Vidya School in Petaluma, California, who started a club to save the elephant. And Andy Holleman, who stopped a developer from building on wetlands. And Kevin Bell, who cleaned up an irrigation drain and saved a bunch of fleas and snails. Finally, you'll meet Clinton Hill, a young Minnesotan whose dedication to saving the Earth has inspired thousands of kids around the world.

Right now, people are making choices about the environment that will affect your future. You could be helping to make those decisions. It's your world, too.

# HOW TO START A
# SAVE THE ENVIRONMENT CLUB

What's your favorite environmental cause?  Protecting wildlife?  Preventing pollution?  Teaching others to respect the Earth?  Whatever you choose, you can be more effective if you join forces with friends.  (There's power in numbers.)  Follow these steps to start a club to promote your cause or project.

1. Find other kids or people who are interested in your cause or project.

2. Plan a place and time to meet.

3. Find an adult adviser for your club.

4. Choose officers for your club:  a president, secretary, treasurer, and anyone else you need.

5. Choose a name for your club.

6. Draw and vote on a logo or symbol for your club.

7. Decide on a project to tackle.

8. Research your project.  Become experts.  Find out as much information as you can.  Identify problems you want to solve.  Interview people.  Survey your neighbors for opinions.

9. Contact state or national groups who might be interested in your ideas.  Ask how you might help them.  Tell them how they might help you.  Build a bigger team.

10. Fundraise for money to support your club.  You can ask for dues, sell goods or services, or request contributions or donations.  Put your money in a bank for safekeeping.

**11.** You may decide to incorporate into a non-profit club so you don't have to pay taxes on your earnings, and so people who give you money don't have to pay taxes on their donations. Here's what to do:

**a.** Contact your Department of Commerce or Secretary of State (or similar office) to file your *articles of incorporation.* You'll report your name, how long you plan to have a club, your purpose, your club logo (symbol), and so on.

**b.** You must get a *business license* with the city or county where you'll be doing business. Contact the business licensing division. Tell them what you plan to do, and they'll point you toward the right department.

**c.** Contact the *Internal Revenue Service (IRS)* to learn the guidelines for becoming a non-profit organization and for obtaining a federal I.D. (identification) number.

**d.** If you want to become a tax-exempt organization (so donations to your group will be tax-free), you'll have to make a special request to the IRS.

**e.** Your adult adviser can help you check your *State Code* for specific details. All main libraries have enormous volumes of your *State Code*, in which you can literally get lost! Ask a librarian to help you find the one that explains how to incorporate.

# STARTING A CLUB TO SAVE THE ELEPHANTS

***Elephants are big. Second-graders are small. But that didn't stop the Fowlers.***

Most second-graders keep busy learning to pass out papers and to write their own names. In 1982, the second-graders at Vidya Elementary School in Petaluma, California, got interested in something bigger. Much bigger. Elephant-sized.

They were listening to their teacher, Diana Lightman, read aloud from a book called *Among the Elephants.* Authors Iain and Oria Douglas-Hamilton painted colorful word pictures of huge gray bodies, "ears flapping like stiff blankets...a row of trunks waving sinuously in a snake dance." The kids sat hypnotized by Mrs. Lightman's mellow voice.

Their teacher told them that 800,000 elephants were killed each year. "At that rate," she said, "it won't take too long before the world won't have any left." She turned a page. "And the worst part is that most of the elephants are killed by poachers, or people who are paid to kill animals illegally for their tusks."

The students learned that elephant poachers sliced off the ivory tusks and left the mutilated carcasses to rot on the ground. In addition, because of overcrowding, the governments of Africa sometimes shot whole herds of elephants.

The children were natural animal lovers. As they listened, their eyes widened and their stomachs churned. Shy, quiet Mark Quirt went home that day, secretly buried his head in his pillow, and cried.

When Mrs. Lightman finished the unit on elephants, the kids weren't ready to quit. They asked Mark's dad, Steve Quirt, to help them form their own wildlife club. They wanted to name it "Friends Of Wild Life," or FOWL for short.

Calling themselves "the Fowlers," the kids slapped paint, snipped with scissors, glued, and drew, creating a slide show, a book, a calendar, and a puppet show about the importance of elephants. Then they put everything in a package and mailed it to the authors of *Among the Elephants* in Kenya, Africa.

"What can we do to help the elephants?" they wondered. Nobody knew. But the kids didn't stop. Even without a project, they plunged ahead.

"For any project, we needed bucks," computer genius Chris Harvey says. "We brainstormed ways to make money and tried them one by one.

"We started small. We focused mainly on bake sales and shoe shines. Our first major way of earning money was to design an elephant poster and get it printed. We took it to a local fair and tried to sell copies. It was a washout. People just weren't interested in wildlife."

Chris began immediately to type up a newsletter to tell other children about elephants. It wouldn't raise money, but it might help to spread their ideas. He also began typing letters for people to sign which called for an ivory ban. If ivory were banned, people couldn't transport it to other countries to sell, and not as many elephants would be killed.

The Fowlers continued to meet once or twice a week. "Sometimes our meetings were a real drag," Forrest Larson remembers, stretching out his long legs. "So we'd tell ourselves, 'It's a dirty job, but somebody's got to do it.'"

In 1986, when the Fowlers were in sixth grade, they finally discovered a good elephant project. And it didn't start with other people who loved the elephants, like they did. It began with a whole tribe that was fed up with elephants.

To the Masai tribe of Kenya, Africa, elephants were a pain. They raided and trampled the Masai's crops. As

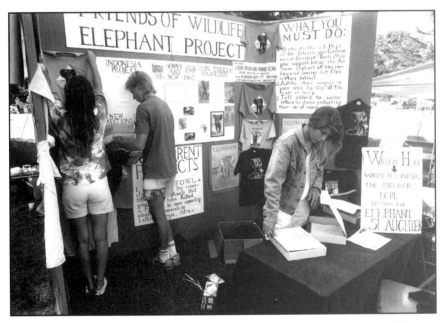

**FOWL kids operate a booth to raise money for elephants.** Photo by Steve Quirt.

a result, the angry farmers speared 20 to 30 elephants every year.

Dr. David Western, a Kenyan citizen and Director of the New York Zoological Society, gave the Fowlers an idea. Maybe an electric fence would keep the elephants away from the Masai's crops. If the kids could raise enough money to buy an electric generator, they could help the Masai government, the farmers, and elephants, too. But the generator would cost $2,000, a lot of money for kids to raise.

The Fowlers met and argued about how to do it.

"It's too much."

"We made posters before. Nobody wanted them."

As the kids disagreed, Forrest remembers, "the room was transformed into a disorganized bunch of screaming members." He laughs. "Erasers and books flew through the air!"

"Look," Chris yelled, "if you really want to change a situation, your heart must be in it. You can't just say, 'Hey man, let's fix the ozone layer,' and then go on with your daily life expecting a change. This is going to take a lot of work."

An eraser hit him on the nose. Then two. Everyone roared. Rama Ruppenthal rolled on the floor, his legs kicking in the air.

"You guys are acting like babies," Melanie Quirt chided them. She picked up the erasers and lined them up on the table. "There are lots of ways that kids can express the power they have. Some kids rebel and leave home. Some scream and throw tantrums." She glared at the others. She was the oldest and tallest of the Fowlers, and she demanded attention. "But we kids in FOWL should use our power to help the world. So settle down!" All at once, she grinned. The gigantic freckles on her face bounced, and everyone relaxed again.

"How about T-shirts?" Steve Quirt asked. "T-shirts with elephants on them? Everyone loves T-shirts. Maybe we could sell those."

And that's what they decided to do. In the beginning, a friendly grandpa showed the kids how to silkscreen the shirts. (Later, they would hire a company to make the shirts for them.) Fowlers took 100 shirts to the Whole Earth Festival in Davis, California. Forrest flexed his muscles and carried at least one-third of the shirts himself.

Rama tossed his pale, shoulder-length hair and threw out a challenge: "Let's have a contest and see who can sell a shirt to the weirdest person." Forrest won hands-down when he sold *three* shirts to a woman wearing a black leopard body stocking, her spiked green hair sprinkled with silver glitter.

While Rama danced through the crowds with shirts to sell, Mark and Chris passed out the form letters asking for an ivory ban. They mailed the signed letters to President Ronald Reagan in Washington, D.C.

The public loved the shirts, and the Fowlers were off and running with a great fundraising project, which they continued for several years. They raised the $2,000 for a solar-powered generator. Quiet Mark, totally dedicated to the project, kept track of the group's money.

"For a moment," Melanie Quirt remembers, "all these people—here and in Africa—were working together for a common cause: helping elephants and humans coexist peacefully. This is an example of how kid power can help the world."

In 1988, the Fowlers received a letter from a woman in the American Southwest. She wrote that Sunny, an elephant at a small, underfunded zoo, was about to be put to sleep—permanently. Why? Because the zoo could no longer afford to keep him alive.

The average elephant snarfs down 120 pounds of hay and up to 300 pounds of vegetation each day. Feeding Sunny was taking a big bite out of the zoo's budget. They simply didn't have the money anymore.

Plus, Melanie explains, Sunny "acted like a neurotic teenager. He'd butt into fences and throw his water dish. He must have had a bad childhood. At any rate, everyone was sick of him."

The Fowlers flew into action. They gave speeches and sold more shirts, raising the $700 necessary to transport Sunny to Popcorn Park in New Jersey.

Content with his larger living quarters at Popcorn, a reformed Sunny began to control some of his delinquent behavior. (Although he still sprays water at an occasional bystander.)

In 1989, the Fowlers attacked a project in the Laikipia plain, northwest of Africa's Mount Kenya. About 2,300 elephants roamed freely over the plain. Their trumpets echoed through acacia trees, and their feet sent up giant sprays of dust. Ranchers enjoyed sharing the land with elephants, because the huge creatures cleared brush and uprooted trees. This allowed new grass to grow and trees to sprout, giving livestock fertile ground for grazing.

Farmers, however, shook their heads in angry disagreement. Elephants barged through their fields and smashed their crops. The farmers couldn't force the elephants to alter their migratory routes and go *around* their fields.

Enter the Fowlers. They raised another $2,000 to help Dr. David Western and *Among the Elephants* author, Iain Douglas-Hamilton, research a solution. The kids offered an idea of their own: Why not build corridors to lead the animals through ranch land, but prevent them from entering farm land?

One day, the group met to discuss their progress so far. "Think about what this has taught us," Melanie said, rubbing the freckles on her arms. "It has taught us skills, like public speaking and organizing. And it has brought us together." She looked around at the other Fowlers.

Rama leaned over and gently punched Chris's shoulder. Chris grinned and slapped Mark and Forrest on their shoulders.

"It was difficult to get all the materials together for fairs," Rama remembered. "Think of all the displays of letters and things for the tables...."

"And Forrest hauling tons of our elephant T-shirts around," Melanie smiled.

"But I think the most difficult part has been to keep us all motivated over the years," Rama offered. "We had to stick with our goals." Nobody laughed, so he continued. "My dream is to see the whole world put back together again the way it was a few hundred years ago." The others nodded their agreement.

In September, 1989, the Fowlers were thrilled to learn that President George Bush had voted for the ivory ban, along with other nations in the U.N. The ban would take effect starting January 1, 1990.

The kids cheered, slapped high-fives, and tackled each other on the floor. Over the years, they had mailed over 1,000 letters to Washington in support of the ban. Now no one could legally hunt or export ivory. More elephants would be saved.

Earlier in 1989, the Fowlers had received an even greater surprise when Oria Douglas-Hamilton came to the United States. Because she was internationally famous for her writing and for living among the elephants, she was scheduled to meet with Barbara Bush, other dignitaries, and news reporters. But Oria said that the most important group she had to meet with was the FOWL kids.

She flew to California, and in a meeting at the San Francisco Academy of Science, Oria asked the children to stand. She told her audience that over the years, whenever she became depressed about the world's ignorance of the elephant's plight, she dug out the worn, original package from the FOWL kids. She looked through the squiggly, second-grade drawings of elephants, the slide show, the calendar, and the handwritten letters on faded school paper. She knew that on the other side of the world, some young children cared. And that, she said, always gave her courage.

The audience applauded for a full three minutes. The Fowlers blinked their eyes and squeezed each other's hands. Then they gave Oria another $1,000 check to keep going.

**FOWL kids pose with the elephants that they have helped to save.** Photo by Steve Quirt.

# SAVING THE WETLANDS

*Andrew Holleman had practically grown up on the wetlands. He loved its plants, creatures, and gooey mud. Then he heard about the developer's plan.*

One day in 1987, Andy Holleman's family received a letter from a land developer. The letter announced the developer's plans to build 180 condominium units near the Hollemans' home in Chelmsford, Massachusetts.

Twelve-year-old Andy snatched the letter and shouted, "He can't do that! He's talking about building right on top of the wetlands!"

Andy knew that several species living on that land were either endangered or on the Special Concern list of animals whose numbers are shrinking. He had spent much of his free time roaming the area, watching great blue herons bend their long, delicate legs in marshy waters, seeing blue-spotted salamanders slither past shy wood turtles, and hearing the red-tailed hawk's lonely call—*cree, cree.* He often ripped off his baseball cap and waved to salute their graceful flight.

"Mom, you've got to take me to the library," Andy insisted. "I need to find out everything I can about the land. We've got to fight this."

143

Cheryl Holleman, a school nurse, dropped her son off at the library. There Andy examined the master plan for their town. He dug into the Annotated Laws for the state. And he discovered that the condos would take up 16.3 acres of land, one-half of which would cover and destroy the wetlands. A new sewage treatment plant, oil from driveways, and fertilizer runoff could all pollute the water system or penetrate the soil, contaminating both water and land.

**Andrew Holleman.** Photo courtesy of Cheryl and David Holleman.

Andy also learned that the proposed development sat on a stream which led into Russell Mill Pond. The pond fed into town wells. So it was possible that Chelmsford's drinking water could be contaminated, too. "Our drinking water was already terrible enough," Andy says, grinning.

He had his ammunition, and he had to do *something*. He thought of all the living things whose habitats would be destroyed by the condos: the ladyslippers, mountain laurels, fringed gentians, foxes, and snakes. And he knew he could count on his parents' support. They had always encouraged him to respect the environment.

Even now, when Cheryl needs Andy to do a chore, she doesn't bother looking for him in front of the TV. She knows she'll find him sprawled half off his bed or stretched across the floor, reading. Andy devours Audubon books about wildlife. He loves author Gerald Durrell's *The Drunken Forest* and *Birds, Beasts, and Other Relatives.* Sometimes, of course, he sneaks in a Stephen King thriller.

Andy and his family have taken many nature walks in the wooded area by Russell Mill Pond. It's something they enjoy doing together—Andy, Cheryl, his dad, David, and his younger brother and sister, Nicholas and Elizabeth.

Andy remembers sitting on the glacial rocks by the stream in the middle of winter, eating baloney sandwiches. In the warmer months, he and Nicholas and Elizabeth played tag in the stream, jumping on the slippery rocks, soaking their shoes, socks, and jeans. When fall came, they gathered brilliant red leaves from swamp maples and golden oak, while their mother picked dried grape vines for wreathes. The children took their leaves home, pressed them between waxed paper, ironed them flat, then hung them on doorknobs and from picture frames.

The wetlands area where the developer wanted to build held other memories for Andy. Sometimes he ice-skated on the pond. Sometimes he made important discoveries.

"Once I brought home a huge baby crow," he says. "A baby crow is called a 'fledgling,' and this one was just learning to fly. It had fallen out of the nest. So I fed him popcorn and water that night, and built him a perch.

"Mom wouldn't let me keep him in the house while I was at school. But that was okay. He was able to fly away the next day to return to his home in the swamp."

When Andy was eleven, he found a skunk caught in a steel-jaw trap, the kind that rips animals' legs apart. Since he had been swimming with a friend, Andy was

wearing only his swim trunks and tattered sneakers—
luckily, as it turned out.

He put on a diving mask, sneaked up behind the
skunk, pressed the release button on the trap, and
grabbed the startled skunk by the tail. Then he carried
him upside-down for a quarter of a mile—all the way to
his house. He knew that skunks can't spray when held
by the tail.

Small children trailed behind him, holding their
noses and giggling. A neighbor telephoned Andy's
mother and said, "Go outside and watch. And shut your
windows and doors behind you. Don't ask me to
explain. Just do it."

By the time Andy arrived home, he was leading
twenty dancing, squealing children, like the Pied Piper.
The skunk dangled from his hand at arm's length.

"This is one animal you're not going to keep,
Andrew," his mom called in a shrill voice.

His father, who was home from his job as a medical
technologist, phoned the local animal shelter for advice.

"They said we could either let the skunk go in the
woods, or bring it in to the shelter," David Holleman told
his son. "You'd better let him go and let nature take its
course. There is no way you're putting that animal in
my car, and you certainly can't hold him out the window
by his tail the whole way to the shelter."

"I let him go," Andy recalls. "His leg wasn't too bad,
so it would probably heal by itself. Everyone thought I
smelled pretty skunky, though. I bathed in vinegar,
which smelled just as awful as the skunk to me. I finally
came clean, but we had to throw my sneakers away."

Crows and skunks aren't the only creatures Andy
has brought home from the wetlands. "My mother
remembers an eighteen-inch snapping turtle which went
to the bathroom all over the kitchen linoleum." He
laughs. "I fed him raw hamburger."

Often Andy just wandered through the woods to think or to write a poem. Sometimes he sat quietly for hours, studying animal behavior. He spotted deer and red foxes. He captured salamanders, snakes, mice, and moles; after learning all he could from observing each animal, Andy carefully carried it back to its home in the woods.

The wetlands were too important to cover with concrete and steel. Andy couldn't allow Pontiacs and Toyotas to replace blue herons and shy wood turtles. He couldn't permit blaring car horns to muffle the *cree* of the red-tailed hawk.

"So I drafted a petition for the residents to sign to try to stop the developer from building," Andy says. "I walked around the neighborhood and collected 180 signatures. I told everyone to come to the public town meeting scheduled with the developer. I also collected about fifty signatures from students in the neighborhood and at McCarthy Middle School."

Only one or two people refused to sign the petition. "They acted like they thought I was too young, like I didn't know what I was doing. But almost everybody was really supportive."

Often Andy carried his petition around for an hour and collected only a few signatures—not because people didn't want to sign, but because they wanted to talk. They'd offer Andy a Coke and invite him in to discuss the problem. Andy spent a lot of time conversing with his neighbors.

An elderly lady named Agatha answered her door with long, bony fingers. Although she was wizened and thin with wild, white hair, Andy's enthusiasm breathed new life into her. She attended over forty meetings and became a real activist.

Once, on the way back from carrying his petition, Andy decided to detour through the swamp. He kicked

up his heels with too much energy and tripped over a
rotted log. He snatched helplessly at the pages of his
petition as they tumbled into a muddy stream, but he
managed to salvage them.

"It took a while for the pages to dry out," he recalls
with a grin, "and then my mom had to iron them out flat.
That's the last time I ever went through the swamp with
something that wasn't waterproofed."

Andy sent copies of his petition to the Board of
Selectmen, the Conservation Commission, the Zoning
Board of Appeals, the Board of Health, and the land
developer. He wrote letters to senators, representatives,
and a TV anchor woman. Although he received letters of
support in return, no one did anything to help.

"When I called the Massachusetts Audubon Society
and told them my problem with the wetlands and that no
one was really helping me, the woman gave me no sym-
pathy," Andy says. "She just told me, 'That's no excuse
for *you*,' and went right on giving information. I learned
that when you really believe in something, you have to
stand up for it no matter how old you are."

Slowly, Andy's neighbors joined in, neighbors he
had contacted with his petition. They organized into the
Concord Neighborhood Association and raised $16,000 to
hire a lawyer and an environmental consultant to fight
the development of the wetlands.

On the night of the town meeting with the developer, over 250 people showed up. The meeting had to be
moved to the basement of the Town Hall to make room
for the crowd. And when the developer stood up and
announced that *he* was the one who had invited everyone, the residents disagreed, saying, "No, it was Andy
Holleman who invited us here."

Andy had prepared a speech to give at the meeting.
When it was time for him to speak, his stomach flipped,

but he walked to the front of the room anyway, brandishing the brown shell of a wood turtle.

"You call yourself the Russell Mill Pond Realty Trust, Inc.," Andy began. "I don't understand how you can call yourself this when you're essentially polluting your own name." The residents responded with thunderous applause. White-haired Agatha winked at him and motioned a thumbs-up.

Andy continued. "We need the wetlands to prevent flooding and to purify the water through the mud," he said. "We need the plants and the creatures living there."

Nobody won that night's debate. In fact, the meetings continued for ten months. There were at least two meetings every week and sometimes more. Andy and either his mom or his dad attended every meeting—and Andy *still* got high grades in school. He spoke at most of the meetings.

In one meeting with the Board of Health, the developer arose and announced, "I'm not going to argue hydro-geological facts with a thirteen-year-old!" Andy's parents were angry, but Andy just shrugged his shoulders.

Nine months after the first meeting, an important test called a "deep-hole test" was conducted in the swamp. The purpose of the test was to find out how quickly a hole dug in the swamp would fill up with water. If it filled up very fast, that would be a sign that the land was not suitable for building.

The developer, members of the Concord Neighborhood Association, and state environmental officials gathered to observe the test. The hole was dug—and it filled with water almost immediately. Andy grinned clear around his head.

The developer tried to withdraw his application to build on the wetlands, but the Zoning Board of Appeals wouldn't let him. Legally, that wouldn't have solved the problem. Someone else could have applied for the same kind of project, and Andy and his neighbors would have had to start fighting all over again. Instead, the Board totally denied the application. Their refusal prevented anyone from trying to build a big development on the wetlands.

When they got the news, Andy and the Concord Neighborhood Association cheered. Their battle was over! And the wetlands were safe from large developers.

Soon after, the developer started building condos on an old drive-in movie lot—an acceptable site Andy had suggested in the beginning.

What did all of this mean to Andy? He became a celebrity. Even though he is modest and shy, he accepted invitations to speak at schools, community groups, and organizations. He received many awards, including the Young Giraffe Award for young people who "stick their necks out" for the good of others. His award was a free trip to the Soviet Union in July, 1990.

And what is Andy doing now? He's planning to go to college in a few years, where he'd like to study environmental law. Meanwhile, he's setting up a non-profit, tax-exempt fund to purchase the wetlands and any surrounding threatened land to preserve it forever. Then he can always wander by Russell Mill Pond, gathering autumn leaves from crimson swamp maples and golden oaks. He can watch the blue herons bend their long, delicate legs in marshy waters, and see blue-spotted salamanders slither safely past shy wood turtles. And he can hear the lonely *cree* of the red-tailed hawk as it soars freely, high above the pond, dipping its wings as if in salute to him. To Andy.

# TESTING THE WATERS

*Beans wouldn't grow in it. Pond snails died in it. There was something wrong with the water in the T.J. drain, and Kevin Bell had the proof in his notebook.*

How would you like to shake hands with the President of the United States? Or, better yet, have your picture taken with him? Sound like an impossible dream? For most of us, it is.

But Kevin Bell, a twelve-year-old boy in Fallon, Nevada, pictured it in his head. He prayed that he would get to meet the President of the United States. His parents didn't know. It was a crazy dream, locked inside Kevin's imagination. In November, 1990, Kevin's crazy dream came true. And here's how it happened.

If you ask Kevin's mom, Gailen, what kind of kid he is, she'll say, "He's quiet. He talks well, and he likes to study. If you go to a church activity, while the other boys are goofing around, Kevin will be off by himself examining a blade of grass."

His greatest frustration is that some teachers at his school, E.C. Best Elementary, don't understand how quickly he learns. He finishes assignments early and has nothing to study. He's *very* good in math. At the end of sixth grade, he came within 15 points of passing the high-school equivalency test for algebra, without ever opening an algebra book.

"The other kids accept Kevin anyway," Gail explains, "although he does get teased a little bit. But mostly they just look at him with big eyes. And since Kevin's intelligence hasn't gone to his head, he has many friends and gets along well with others."

Kevin is a pack rat, but an organized pack rat. He collects all kinds of things: bugs, coins, arrowheads, fossils, rocks. But he arranges each collection neatly into egg cartons or shoe boxes. His collections decorate his bedroom.

He enjoys sports of all kinds, and plays baseball, soccer, and football. His slim build has helped him win awards for gymnastics, both in his state and regional competitions.

How did he get started on the project which took him to meet the President? It began as an entry in the school science fair. His science teacher, Walter Plants, had encouraged him to enter the fair. Kevin thought he might like to do something with testing water. Someone suggested that he test salt water, but Kevin thought that was too ordinary.

Kevin read in the newspaper that fish and wildlife were dying from contamination at Stillwater, a national wildlife refuge in Nevada. Stillwater is part of the Pacific Flyway, a migratory route for birds. It's bordered by 67,000 acres of farmland, which are irrigated regularly. The irrigation water seeps down into the water table, and 20 huge drains carry it to the Stillwater Refuge. Kevin wondered if one of the drains could be contaminated.

He and his mom visited the refuge and met with Norm Saake, Water Fowl Biologist for the Nevada

Department of Fish and Wildlife. Kevin asked him which of the drains was the worst.

Mr. Saake dragged out a five-gallon bucket and filled it with water from the T.J. drain. "This is the most polluted drain," he said. He gave the water to Kevin.

"The drain was only six years old," Kevin explains. "The new drains are the worst because minerals and salts haven't been flushed out of the soil. The contamination will go away after a bunch of years, but the drain water would kill everything by then."

Next, Kevin met with Ron Anglin, manager of the Stillwater Refuge, who showed him how to conduct a scientific experiment.

Kevin decided to test the T.J. drain water to see if beans could grow in it. As a "control" for his test—something to check it against—he needed some fresh, uncontaminated water, which he collected from the Lahontan Reservoir.

"I wanted to find out how much fresh water to add so that things could live," he explains. "All around the ditch where the T.J. emptied, it looked sort of deserty, with tumbleweeds around. It looked dry, with not many trees or big bushes." Kevin observed that many animals seemed to instinctively stay away from the water.

Kevin carted both water samples home. On February 25, 1990, he planted four beans each in three different pots. Then he watered them with different concentrations of T.J. drainwater and fresh water. The beans in the 100 percent T.J. drainwater didn't even break through the surface of the dirt.

Kevin decided he needed some living creatures to test in the contaminated water. He, his mom, and his little sister, Kallie, went fishing in the Carson River for "volunteers." Because his little sister had a broken arm, she couldn't fish. Pouting in the mud, she decided to grub for snails instead.

"It turned out to be a pretty good idea that she dug up snails," Kevin says, tugging on his Chicago Cubs hat. "Because that gave me an idea. The government hadn't tested snails. So I decided to test them.

"Pond snails are pretty interesting. They don't have to have a mate to make babies. I got them at the right time of year to watch them reproduce. You could see eggs in a jelly mass at the sides of my jars."

Kevin tested the creatures he had collected. Mosquito Fish started dying after 96 hours in 100 percent T.J. drainwater. Sacramento Black Fish died in less than five hours.

Pond snails died in just five minutes.

Clearly, T.J. drainwater was not a fun place to be if you were a pond creature.

**Kevin experiments with T.J. drainwater.** Photo courtesy of James Bell.

Kevin also tested some microscopic organisms and Daphnia water fleas. The fleas didn't like the 100 percent T.J. drainwater at all. They all died within five *seconds*.

Next, Kevin wanted to test the fleas with diluted T.J. drainwater. But his family had planned to go to Palm Springs to visit Kevin's grandmother. No problem; Kevin took the fleas with him in the car, along with the fish and the pond snails.

Everyone took turns babysitting the fleas. Since they had to be checked every few hours, Kevin's mom and dad even took shifts in the night. "The only bad part is, I spilled some of my Daphnia on my grandma's kitchen floor," Kevin grins.

The Daphnia experiments yielded some interesting results. While fleas in 100 percent T.J. water died almost immediately, fleas in 50 percent T.J. water lived for an hour and fifteen minutes. Fleas in 25 percent T.J. water lived for four days.

Kevin's experiments convinced everyone that the T.J. drainwater was hazardous to the health of pond creatures. His project took first place at the Nevada State Science Fair. His notebook told how he had carefully tested his theories for two and one-half months.

But Kevin's project didn't end with the Science Fair. Before long, other people grew very interested in his test results. It all started when Kevin's mother showed his notebook to Ron Anglin at the Stillwater Refuge.

Ron was amazed. Twelve-year-old Kevin had obtained the same results with his simplified tests, which cost about $25, as government officials had reported in their own 55-page study, which cost about $30,000!

Ron asked Mrs. Bell for permission to photocopy her son's notebook. Then he took the copy to Bill Bettenburg, assistant to the U.S. Secretary of the Interior. (As Kevin had expected, the government was especially interested in his experiments with pond snails.) From there, Kevin's notebook was entered into the *Congressional Record* on May 8, 1990. He became a part of American history.

Back in Washington, Kevin's work was used by legislative aides to draft a new bill called the Reid Water Bill, after Senator Harry Reid, who initiated it. If the Reid Bill became law, it would end 80 years of water wars in Nevada. It would also close the contaminated T.J. drain.

Meanwhile, since Kevin's research proved that the T.J. drainwater would need to be mixed with 75 percent fresh water to make it habitable, the Nature Conservatory purchased new water for the Stillwater Refuge. On the day the fresh water was added, Kevin helped to open the flood gates. Other dignitaries on hand included Harry Reid and Richard Bryan, the U.S. Senators from Nevada, and John Turner, Director of the U.S. Department of Fish and Wildlife.

But it didn't end there. First, Kevin received the Governor's Conservation Award from Nevada Governor Bob Miller. Then he flew to Washington, D.C., to receive the President's Environmental Youth Award from President George Bush himself.

"I was so excited, I almost threw up," Kevin remembers. But he shook the President's hand and got his autograph. While Kevin was in Washington, President Bush signed the Reid Water Bill into effect, which closed the T.J. drain.

"That was the most amazing moment for me—going to Washington to meet the President," Kevin says, still in awe. "I didn't think it would get this far at all. I was so nervous!"

Kevin doesn't spend too much time reliving his success. Instead, his mind wanders off, already tackling a new project. "My dream now is to find something that will clear the contaminated water. Did you know there's a balance of trace minerals that will make things live in water six times as long...."

# "KIDS FOR SAVING EARTH"

***Thousands of kids around the world keep Clinton Hill's dream alive.***

There's a tree on a small hill by Sunny Hollow Elementary School in Minneapolis, Minnesota. Not a large tree— just a little ash. It's not a tree that would win a blue ribbon, or that someone passing by would even notice.

Planting the tree was sixth grader Dan Springrose's idea. He and his classmates did it in memory of their friend, Clinton Hill, who died of a brain tumor when he was only eleven. Now they call the place where they planted the tree "Clinton's Hill."

But that's not the end. It's only the middle. And you need to hear about Clinton from the beginning.

When Clinton was a toddler, he loved his Big Wheels cycle. He'd spin it in circles and fly off cardboard jumps. At night, he'd bounce into bed with his parents, Tessa and Will, wake them up, and

157

squeak, "It's me!  It's the bed-jumper.  And the foot-snuggler."  Then he'd rub his cold toes up and down their legs.

Clinton loved to talk.  By the time he was six, if he couldn't corner you to listen, he would walk up and hit you.  It wasn't an angry hit.  He just wanted you to know he was there.  And he wanted you to listen—right now!

He'd follow you around, tugging at your sleeve, as he spilled over with imaginary stories of space travel and Star Wars heroes.  His dark eyes sparkled under uneven bangs.  He'd tell you that he had magical powers and then throw his arms around your waist, or pull your head down and give you a hug.

**Clinton Hill, founder of Kids for Saving Earth.**
Photo courtesy of William and Tessa Hill.

As he grew from a toddler into an active little boy, Clinton played Wiffle Ball with his dad.  He also played all the other kid sports:  baseball, basketball, soccer.  But he never really cared very much if his team won or lost.  He played for fun and to be with his friends.

Clinton often asked his dad, "Why are people mean to each other?"  Clinton thought that people should be kind and helpful to everyone, no matter who they were, and give everyone a chance.  In spite of weird looks, he yelled "Hi!" to all the strangers in the shopping malls.

He cracked original jokes, such as: "What's round and red and you can wear it?"  Before you could come up with a clever answer, he'd shout, "A pimple!"  And then he'd bound off laughing.

Clinton drew posters and wrote songs about nature. He worried about pollution.  When he saw a documentary about an endangered species of penguins, he cried. He asked questions about dolphins, too.  Would they be around when he was an old man?  Was there a clock ticking away somewhere?  Was there only a little time left for the Earth if people didn't change?  He told his dad, "Kids will be the ones to teach the adults to take care of the Earth."

Clinton decided, "We can help people change. People are the pollution solution. I'll be a defender of the planet.  To keep the world healthy and beautiful."

One day Clinton told his mother, "I want to start my own club.  I want to call it 'Kids for Saving Earth.'"  He talked with his friends at school and started making plans.

At school, he dreamed about his plans.  He often behaved in an absent-minded way, his glasses slipping down his nose, as he stared into space.  If the teacher or anyone else scolded him for not listening, he would reply in his slightly nasal voice, "It's just that what is going on in my own mind is so much more interesting."

But while Clinton worried about the Earth's future, there was another clock ticking away inside his brain.

In the fall of 1988, he began to show strange symptoms.  He'd wander out of his bedroom at night and walk down the hallway with a disoriented look on his face. He developed headaches and began to vomit.

Tessa and Will grew concerned.  They decided that Clinton needed to see a doctor.  After a CAT Scan at the hospital in December, 1988, they received the shocking news: Clinton was diagnosed as having a malignant brain tumor.

The doctor put him in the hospital that night for tests, and two days later performed a delicate brain operation. In spite of many hours of surgery, the doctor was able to remove only 75 percent of the huge mass in Clinton's brain.

The family remained positive. They fully believed that Clinton would recover. His father, Will, says, "He always kept his sense of humor—through everything."

Clinton never doubted that things would turn out okay. After all, he was the kid with magical powers! A few days after his first surgery, he woke up in the middle of the night and wanted a bath. After the bath, his mom got his clothes ready to help him dress. She said, "Okay, Clinton, I'm going to put your underwear on now." Without hesitating, he answered, "I don't think they'll fit you, Mom."

He began chemotherapy, a process of drinking a solution of chemicals every six weeks to kill the tumor and keep it from spreading. Each time, the process would cause him to vomit and feel "crummy." His dad recalls that Clinton didn't make a big deal out of it. He'd say something like, "Well, if I drink it today, I'll be able to go the carnival by Sunday."

Clinton seemed to recover quickly from the surgery and the chemotherapy. He wanted to start his club. By now, he had decided that it should be an international club. His mother smiled and told him to wait until he was completely well. "We never thought he would really die," she remembers.

Clinton returned to school full time. He had grown thinner. But even with deep hollows in his cheeks, he kept grinning. He thought that his problems were not so bad as those of a friend whose parents were getting a divorce.

He grew anxious to get his club started. One evening, as he sat reading a copy of *Boys' Life* magazine, he found an advertisement in the back for a button-making machine. "What a great idea," he thought. "I could make buttons for my club." He must have felt some sense of urgency, because he snatched his magic markers and drew a poster of a green-and-blue Earth. Under and around it, he wrote, "Kids for Saving Earth, the Pollution Solution. Please give a contribution. Any amount. Put in cup, please. Thank you."

Then he interrupted his parents' dinner party and passed a cup to collect money for the button machine. He collected $4.50. As Tessa and Will tucked him into bed that night, he told them in tired voice that he might need their help to keep the club going. They promised to help.

Clinton's parents wanted the best treatment available for their son. They packed up their family and moved to Houston, Texas, for a few months, where Clinton received a second diagnosis at the M.D. Anderson Cancer Center. Unfortunately, after many tests, the doctors determined that the tumor had grown. It meant a second surgery for Clinton in February, 1989.

Clinton accepted the news calmly. He knew he had to go through it. The second operation went well. "He was phenomenal in his recovery from surgery," his dad remembers. "He was home in just a few days. And he never lost his faculties. He was always alert and maintained his sense of humor. Like the time when he was out flat on the table waiting to receive radiation. He tried to get the doctors to radiate his bubble gum."

Clinton always bantered with one particular doctor, Dr. Woo. One day, when Dr. Woo came into the room, Clinton asked, "Do you have a joke today?" Dr. Woo's eyes wrinkled as he answered, "Do you have to have a joke *every* day?" Then Clinton replied, "You're the only doctor who comes up with any jokes. The rest *are* jokes."

As a result of the radiation, Clinton lost hair on both sides of his head. But he looked at himself in the mirror with a sly grin. "I've got a Mohawk now," he told his parents.

Back in school, he simply wore a baseball hat. Once, as he waited in a line to buy a 25 cent snow cone from the PTA, he overheard two boys whispering. "Will you loan me a quarter if I show you something neat?" one boy said. The second boy nodded. Pointing at Clinton, the first boy said, "That kid over there has a Mohawk." Overhearing the conversation, Clinton tipped his hat so all could see his hair. Everyone laughed, including Clinton, and the first kid got his quarter for a snow cone.

Clinton continued to improve. At the same time, his parents researched every possible cure they could find, including changing his diet and using positive thinking and visualization. The whole family was convinced that Clinton would fully recover. They set out for a much needed vacation to Colorado.

Their week-long vacation expanded into four weeks as they continued on to the Grand Canyon and Disneyland. While they drove along, they sang "Zippety Doo Dah." Each day was more wonderful than the last, simply because it was so great being together. Clinton added his usual dose of homemade humor: "What's red, yellow, and green and makes you want to scream?" He threw out his arms. "A traffic light!"

When they returned home to Minnesota, Clinton, Will, and Karina grabbed the Wiffle Ball and headed for the backyard. "Clinton could really smack that ball," his dad remembers.

"By September, Clinton could still hit, but he stopped running around the bases," Will says. "He grew tired. His legs wobbled beneath him." Clinton's dad pauses, clears his throat, and then continues. "Soon we didn't go out at all."

"This was a special kid," said Paul Tesdahl, principal at Sunny Hollow School. "In those last months, you knew he was hurting. He'd miss a few days of school, then you'd see him in the hall, and he'd have this big smile. He'd say, 'Hey, Mr. T., how ya' doin'?'"

On Thanksgiving Day, Clinton sat with his family around the carved turkey and cranberries. They shared with one another all the things they were grateful for. When it was his turn to speak, Clinton said, "I'm grateful for my family and all my wonderful friends."

Four days later, on November 27, 1989, the kid with magical powers slipped away. His father, Will, was with him at the end. He doesn't like to talk about it. He isn't certain exactly which moment Clinton died. He just sort of slipped away, like a puff of smoke.

The funeral was attended by many of Clinton's friends, teachers, and adults. As his parents pulled themselves together following the funeral, they set about fulfilling their promise to Clinton to keep his club going.

Tessa and Will went to Sunny Hollow Elementary School and began formally organizing Kids for Saving Earth. Target Stores, a large chain of department stores based in Minnesota, heard of their plans and adopted the project. Adults met with kids, and kids brainstormed what they wanted to do. The fourth-grade club raised $50 and bought an acre of forest in the Children's International Rain Forest in Costa Rica so it couldn't be destroyed. They also adopted a whale.

Clinton's parents designed club buttons from Clinton's drawings and handwriting, made stickers, and printed T-shirts. They began a newsletter for kids. Clinton's parents wrote a song and a promise using Clinton's ideas and words.

Target Stores financed a massive mailing to inform other children about starting their own environmental KSE—Kids for Saving Earth—clubs. New clubs sprang up all over the United States and Canada. A child from the Soviet Union wrote for information on how to start one over there.

Clinton's friends went to the United Nations Youth Environment Forum in May, 1990, and told the 2,000 children there about Clinton's dream. They gave T-shirts to every child present, and the audience sang their song.

When Soviet President Mikhail Gorbachev and his wife, Raisa, visited Minnesota in June, 1990, KSE sang their song and presented them with buttons and T-shirts.

It started small, with the simple dream of a ten-year-old boy and a cup with $4.50 in it. And a hill with an ash tree on it. Now there are over 1,300 KSE clubs and 30,000 members, including chapters in such faraway places as Ireland, Costa Rica, and the Soviet Union. There's a newsletter that has reached over thirty-five *million* people. Letters pour in every day with reports from club members around the world.

KSE kids are recycling and influencing parents to make changes. They're marching in parades, collecting litter, and planting trees across the country. They're adopting endangered species, saving beaches, fighting in their communities for clean air....And that's only the beginning.

# INDEX

## A

Acid rain, 131
Advertising
 anti-crime, 11
 for social action, 53
Africa, elephants in, 136, 137-138, 140
After-school programs, 28-32
AIDS Prevention Committee (Mass.), 30
Alcohol, avoiding, 8
American Search Dogs, 119
*Among the Elephants* (Douglas-Hamilton), 135, 136, 140
Anasazi Indian culture, 56
Ancestors, 56, 59-64
Anderson (M.D.) Cancer Center (Houston, Tex.), 161
Anglin, Ron, 153, 155
Animal behavior, studying, 147
Animals, saving, 136-142, 143-150, 152-156
Annotated Laws, 144
Archaeology, 56
Articles of incorporation, for non-profit clubs, 133
Assault, 7
Athletic and Good Sportsmanship Award, 116
Atlas, as hero, 89
Audubon books, 145

## B

Bear Dance, 63
Bell, Kevin, 131, 151-156
Bennett, William, 30
Best (E.C.) Elementary School (Fallon, Nev.), 151
Bettenburg, Bill, 155
*Birds, Beasts, and Other Relatives* (Durrell), 145
Boca Raton, Fla., 63
Boney, Carl, 90, 99-103
Boston Against Drugs, 30
 rally, 32
Boston University, 32
Boy Scouts, 75, 100, 102, 117
 Native American, 63
Boys Club, 11, 14
*Boys' Life* magazine, 161
Brain tumor, 160
Bravery, 89. *See also* Heroism
Breakdancing class, 75
Breast cancer, 70
Bryan, Richard, 156
Buckhorn Mine (Stockton, Utah), 122
Buddy system, to avoid crime, 8
Burke (Jeremiah E.) High School (Dorchester, Mass.), 28
Bus fares, lower kids', 65-66
Bush, Barbara, 141
Bush, George, 96, 127, 141, 156

Business license, for non-profit
     clubs, 133
Butternut Mountain (Mass.), 28
Buttons, as fundraiser, 161, 163

## C

California Governor's Award, 96
Cancer, 70, 159-164
Carson, Charles, 7, 11-17
Carson River (Nev.), 153
Castro, Barbara, 7, 35-36, *37*
CAT scan, 159
Catholic church, 114
CBS National News, 11
Ceremonies, Native American,
     57
Chelmsford, Mass., 143
Chemotherapy, 160
Chicago Cubs, 79
Chicago, Ill., 41
Child molesting. *See* Sexual abuse
Children's International Rain
     Forest (Costa Rica), 163
Children's programs, funding
     for, 69
Christensen, Gary, 123
City council, testifying before, 68
Citywide Youth Congress
     (Mass.), 30
Clairol Corporation, 78
Clark, Melinda, 90, 105-110
Cleveland (Grover) Middle
     School (Dorchester, Mass.),
     28
"Clinton's Hill," 157
Cliques, 82
Clubs
     non-profit, 133
     starting, 132-133, 136-142,
          159-164
Cocaine. *See* Drugs
Collections, 152
Colors, learning, 74-75
Commitment, 3, 131

Community hearings, testifying
     at, 68
Community service, 16, 51
Concord Neighborhood
     Association (Chelmsford,
     Mass.), 148
*Congressional Record, The*, 155,
     167
Conservation. *See* Environment
Control, 3
Costa Rica
     KSE clubs in, 164
     rain forest in, 163
Counseling
     for drug abuse, 14
     peer, 37, 69-70
     for sexual abuse, 24
     teen hotline, 69-70
Courage, 90, 127, 131. *See also*
     Faith
"Coyote and Its Reflection, The"
     (folk tale), 63
Creativity, 131
Creator, communicating with,
     57. *See also* God
Crime
     anti-crime organization, 34
     avoiding, 8-9
     fighting, 7-48
     neighborhood, 28
     reporting, 9, 20
     in schools, 33-39
     victims, 7-9
Curfew, for teenagers, 68

## D

Daily, Frank, 51, 81-85
D'Alesio, Andy, 90, 111-116
Dance clubs, teen, 68-69
Davis, Calif., 139
Deafness, 74-79
Deep-hole test, 149
Dehydration, 124
Dennis, Joshua, 3, 90, 117-128

Diet, and cancer, 162
Disabled youth, helping, 77
Dorchester, Mass., 27
Douglas-Hamilton, Iain, 135, 140
Douglas-Hamilton, Oria, 135, 141
Drowning, 111-116
Drugs
  addiction, 12
  avoiding, 8
  fighting, 11-17, 29, 38-39
  overdose of, 27
  speaking against, 29
Drunken Forest, The (Durrell),
  145
Dry Canyon (Utah), 121
Dukakis, Michael, 30
Dunbar High School (Miami,
  Fla.), 47
Duncan, Clifford, 56-59
Duncan, Jenna, 51, 55-56, 60-64
Duncan, John, 58, 59-64
Duncan, Rena, 51, 55-64
Durrell, Gerald, 145

E

E.C. Best Elementary School
  (Fallon, Nev.), 151
ECHO. See Exploited Children's
  Help Organization (ECHO)
Elephants
  saving, 135-142
  starting a club to save, 131,
  135-142
Elders. See Ancestors
Emerson, Ralph Waldo, on
  heroes, 89
Endangered species, saving,
  135-142, 143-150
Environment
  clubs, 132-133
  respect for, 144
  saving, 131-164
Environmental law, 150
Etowski, Michael, 90, 99-103

Everett, Penn., 105
"Everybody's Got to Have a
  Hero" (song), 126
Experiments, for testing water,
  152-156. See also Science
  fairs
Exploited Children's Help
  Organization (ECHO), 25
Extinction, of species, 131

F

Faith, 120, 126, 127, 128. See also
  Courage
Fallon, Nev., 151
Family, dysfunctional, 12
Fayetteville, North Carolina, 99
Fears, overcoming, 90
Federal identification number,
  for non-profit clubs, 133
Fighting, preventing, 37-38
Fire, 105-110
Flashbacks, 19, 24, 25
Flynn, Raymond, 30
Foster homes, 12
Foundation for Exceptional
  Children, 78
FOWL/Fowlers. See Friends of
  Wild Life (FOWL)
Friends of Wild Life
  (FOWL/Fowlers), 136-142
Frostbite, 124
Fulton, Missouri, 76
Fundraising, 53, 69, 132, 136,
  137, 138-139, 140, 161, 163

G

Gandhi, as hero, 89
Gangs, 3, 15, 16, 42-48
Garcia, Jess, 120
Geronimo, as hero, 89
Giraffe Project, 47, 150

Girl Scouts
   International Festival, 113
   Native American, 63
Girls Club, 14
God, belief in, 12, 14. *See also*
   Creator
Gorbachev, Mikhail, 164
Gorbachev, Raisa, 164
Governor's Conservation Award
   (Nev.), 156
Graffiti, reporting, 36
Grover Cleveland Middle School
   (Dorchester, Mass.), 28
Gun control, 3, 91-97
Gutierrez, Lazaro, 35
Guyman, Ray, 123

## H

Habitats, saving, 144
Handicapped groups, limitations
   of, 75-77
Harvey, Chris, 136
Hearing impairment, 74-79
Heber Valley (Utah), 59, 62
Henderson, Kathleen, 93
Hercules, as hero, 89
Heroism, 85, 89-90, 91-128
   characteristics of, 90
Hidden Treasure Mine
   (Stockton, Utah), 117-128
Hill, Clinton, 131, 157-164
History fair, 58
Hitchhiking, and avoiding
   crime, 8
Holland Elementary School
   (Dorchester, Mass.), 29
Holleman, Andy, 47, 131,
   143-150
Hope (John) School (Chicago,
   Ill.), 42, 44-45, 48
Houston, Tex., 161
Howard University, 38

## I

"I Am a Child of God" (song), 126
Indian Reorganization Act, 62
Instincts, using to avoid crime, 8
Internal Revenue Service (IRS),
   guidelines for non-profit
   clubs, 133
Ireland, KSE clubs in, 164
Irrigation drains, 131, 152
IRS. *See* Internal Revenue
   Service (IRS)
Ivory elephant tusks, 136, 137,
   139, 141

## J

Jackson, Jesse, 32
James, Donna, 71
Jenkins, Ted, Dr., 124
Jeremiah E. Burke High School
   (Dorchester, Mass.), 28
Jesus, as hero, 89
John Hope School (Chicago, Ill.),
   42, 44-45, 48
Jones, Mercedes (pseudonym),
   7, 19-26
Jordan, Michael, as hero, 89

## K

Kennedy, Edward (Ted), 30, *31*,
   70
Kennedy Park (Reynoldsburg,
   Ohio), 116
Kenya, Africa, 136, 137
Kid power, 138, 139
Kids for Saving Earth (KSE)
   clubs, 157-164
*Kid's Guide to Social Action, The*
   (Lewis), 167
Kids in Court (ECHO program),
   25-26
Kidsboard (Seattle, Wash.), 68, 69

Killings, 7
  drug-related, 12
  gang, 42-44
  of students, 33, 42-44
King, Martin Luther, Jr., as
    hero, 89
KSE. *See* Kids for Saving Earth
    (KSE)

**L**

Lahontan Reservoir (Nev.), 153
Laikipia plain (Africa), elephants
    in, 140
Land development, 143-150
Larson, Forrest, 137
Leadership, 69
Lee Elementary School
    (Dorchester, Mass.), 30
Letters, 137, 139, 141, 142
Lewis, Barbara A., 167
  address, 4
Libraries, 133, 143
Lightman, Diana, 135, 136
Little Haiti Subcouncil for
    Crime Prevention (Miami,
    Fla.), 38
Long, Samuel, 51, 73-79
Louisville, Kentucky, 19

**M**

Madison Park High School
    (Dorchester, Mass.), 29
Marijuana. *See* Drugs
Marquette High School
    (Milwaukee, Wisc.), 82, 85
Masai tribe (Kenya, Africa), 137,
    138
Massachusetts Audubon Society,
    148
McAdoo, Keema, 7, 27-32
McCarthy Middle School
    (Chelmsford, Mass.), 147
McPherson, Bob, 116

M.D. Anderson Cancer Center
    (Houston, Tex.), 161
Media
  anti-crime messages in, 11,
    16-17, 35
  on bus fare protest, 65-66
  children avoiding, 44
  coverage of anti-gang speech,
    47
  coverage of sexual abuse trial,
    22
Medicine man, 59, 61
Memories, blocking, 20, 24
Metabolism
  imbalance of, 74
  and sleep, 124
Miami, Fla., 33
Miami (Fla.) Metro Police, 35
Miller, Bob, 156
Miller, Jerry, 116
Miller, John, 70
Milwaukee, Wisc., 81
Mine
  exploring, 117-119
  lost in, 3, 119-128
Minneapolis, Minn., 131, 157
Missouri School for the Deaf, 76
Mormon church, 120, 127
Mother Teresa, as hero, 89
Motivation, 141
Mount, Jack, 97
Murder. *See* Killings
Murray, Dallas, 60
Museum for the Ute Indian
    Tribe, 56
Myton Elementary School
    (Utah), 63

**N**

Nardelli, Vic, 33-37
National Crime Prevention
    Council, 34
National Drug Control Policy,
    Office of, 30

Native American Boy Scouts and
Girl Scouts competition, 63
Native American culture, 56-64
Navajo Indian Tribe, 59
Neola Elementary School (Utah),
56, 63
Nevada Department of Fish and
Wildlife, 152-153
Nevada State Science Fair, 155
New York Zoological Society, 138
Newsletters, 136, 163, 164
Night blindness, 119
Ninja Turtles, as heroes, 89
Non-profit clubs, steps for incor-
poration, 133
Northwest Asian-American
Theater, 66

**O**

Office of National Drug Control
Policy, 30
Ophir Canyon (Utah), 121
Organization skills, 141
Ortega, Ruben, 3, 90, 91-97

**P**

Pacific Flyway (Nev.), 152
Pack rats, 152
Painting, 57
Past, connection with, 59-60
Peer pressure, positive, 34
Perry, Richard, 100, 103
Persistence, 54, 73-79
Petaluma, Calif., 131, 135
Petitions, 137, 139, 147
Petroglyphs, 56
Picketing
against violence, 44
to lower kid's bus fares, 65-66
Plants, Walter, 152
Poachers, elephants killed by,
136

Police
patrolling school, 47
teaching students about
violence, 44
Pollution, 131, 144, 159
Ponds. See Wetlands
Popcorn Park (New Jersey), 140
Positive thinking, and cancer,
162
Posters, as fundraiser, 136, 161
President's Environmental
Youth Award, 156
Problem-solving, inspiration for,
2, 3, 131
Project (Miami, Fla. neighbor-
hood), 35-36
Project Serve (Miami, Fla.), 44,
47
Public speaking
as heroic behavior, 90, 148-149
as skill, 32, 42, 63-64, 141, 150
in speech contest, 44-48
Puppet show, 136

**Q**

Quirt, Mark, 136
Quirt, Melanie, on kid power,
138, 139

**R**

Race relations, 17
Radiation, treatment for cancer,
162
Radio station, and anti-crime
messages, 35
Rain forests, 131, 163
Rambo, as hero, 89
Rape, 7, 26
Rather, Dan, 11
Reagan, Ronald, 139
Reflections, 1, 2
Reid, Harry, 156
Reid Water Bill, 156

Reynoldsburg, Ohio, 111
Rice, Norm, 70, 71
Rifles. *See* Gun control
Rights, kid's, 65-71
Risk-takers, heroes as, 90
Rivera, Julie, 93
Rogers, Fred, 33
Rogers, Will, on heroes, 89
Role models, heroes as, 90
Role playing, 31
Ronan Park (Dorchester, Mass.),
    27, 32
Rosehill Elementary School
    (Reynoldsburg, Ohio), 116
Ruppenthal, Rama, 138
Russell Mill Pond (Chelmsford,
    Mass.), 144-150
Russell Mill Pond Realty Trust,
    Inc., 149

# S

Saake, Norm, 152-153
St. Anne's Catholic School
    (North Carolina), 99
St. Armand, Sandy, 7, 36-39
St. Patrick's Catholic School
    (North Carolina), 100
Salt Lake City, Utah, 58, 61,
    120, 167
Salt Lake Search and Rescue
    Team (Utah), 119
San Francisco Academy of
    Sciences, 142
San Gabriel High School (Calif.),
    91
Santos, Nelson, 35
Save-the-Environment Club,
    steps for starting, 132-133
School bus accident, 99-103
School Resource Police (Miami,
    Fla.), 35
Science fairs, 152, 155
Seattle Central Community
    College, 66

Seattle Metro Center YMCA, 68,
    69
Seattle University, 16
Seattle, Wash., 65
    city board/commissions,
        youth representatives, 70
Seizures, 73
Self-esteem class, 14
Sexual abuse, 19-26
    trial, 21, 22-23
Shimomura, Joby, 51, 65-71
Shock, treatment for, 102
Shootings, in schools, 3, 33,
    42-44, 47, 93-97. *See also*
    Killings
Shoshone Indian Tribe, 59
Sign language, 7477
Silkscreening, 139
Sioux Indian Tribe, 59
Skinner, John, 121-128
Skunks, 145-146
Sleep, and metabolism, 124
Slide show, 136
Smith, Mr. (child molester,
    pseudonym), 20, 21-23, 24
Smith, Norvell, 3, 7, 41-48
Smithsonian Institution
    (Washington, D.C.), 57
Smoke inhalation, 109
Snails, 151, 154, 155
Social action, 51-85
    defined, 51
    tips for taking, 52-54
Soldier Canyon (Utah), 122
Southridge High School (Miami,
    Fla.), 7, 33-39
Soviet Union
    KSE clubs in, 164
    visit to as speech award, 47-48
Spartan Patrol (YCW), 34-39
Special concern list, of animals,
    143
Special Olympics, 77-78
Speech contest, 44-48
Speeches. *See* Public speaking

Spirit of Young American
    Award, 78
Sportsmanship, 112
Springfield, Missouri, 76
Springfield Park Board day camp
    (Springfield, Missouri), 77
*State Code*, on incorporation of
    non-profit clubs, 133
Stealing. *See* Theft
Stickers, as fundraiser, 163
Stillwater Refuge (Nev.), 152, 153
Stockton, Utah, 117
Streams. *See* Wetlands
Street life, 12-13
Sundance ceremony, 57
Sunny (elephant), 139-40
Sunny Hollow Elementary School
    (Minneapolis, Minn.), 157
Superman, as hero, 89
Survival, techniques, 124,
    125-127
Sutcliff, Rick, 79
Swamps. *See* Wetlands
Sweat ceremonies, 57

## T

"Tables Turned, The"
    (Wordsworth), 93
Tacoma Community College, 17
Tacoma, Wash., 11
Tacoma Youth Initiative, 16
Tapp, John D., 96
Target Stores, 163
Tax-exempt, non-profit clubs, 133
Teaching methods, questioning,
    66
Teen Convention, 69
Teen Hotline, 69
Teenagers, as crime victims, 7
Tesdahl, Paul, 163
Theft, 7-9
    drug-related, 12
Threats, 20, 21
*Today Show*, 70

Tooele County Search and
    Rescue Team (Utah), 119
Town meetings, 147, 148-149
Trace minerals, 156
Trial, sexual abuse, 21, 22-23
    testifying at, 21
Truancy rate, 39
T-shirts, as fundraiser, 139, 163,
    164
Turner, John, 156

## U

Uintah Band (Ute Indians), 59, 62
Uintah Mountains (Utah), 55, 57
Uintah Reservation (Utah), 62
Unca Som, *58*, 59-64
United Nations, ivory ban by,
    141
United Nations Youth
    Environment Forum, 164
University of Puget Sound, 17
U.S. Department of Fish and
    Wildlife, 156
U.S. Department of Justice, 116
U.S. Secretary of the Interior,
    155
U.S. Smelting and Mining
    Company, 118
Utah Legislature, 60, 63-64, 167
Utah State Capitol building, 58,
    60-63
Utah Power and Light rescue
    team, 120, 123
Ute Indian Reservation, 60
Ute Indian Tribe, 56-64

## V

Valuables, locking up, 8
Vandalism, 28
Vidya Elementary School
    (Petaluma, Calif.), 131, 135

Violence, 42-44. *See also* Gangs;
    Shootings; Killings
    convention on, 69
    drug-related, 43
Violence Prevention Committee
    (Mass.), 30
Visualization, and cancer, 162

## W

Wake Forest University
    (Winston-Salem, North
    Carolina), 85
Wally, Sergeant, 21, 22, 24
War Dance, 63
Washington Governor's School
    for Citizen Leadership, 16
Water, experiments for testing,
    152-156
Wells, pollution of, 144
Western, David, 138, 140
Wetlands, saving, 131, 143-150,
    152-156
Whitman Middle School
    (Seattle, Wash.), 68
Whole Earth Festival (Davis,
    Calif.), 139
Wiggins, Cheryl, 35
Wildlife, saving, 136-142,
    143-150, 152-156
Williams, John ("Kojak"), 83, *84*
Woo, Dr., 161
Wordsworth, William, 93

## Y

YCW. *See* Youth Crime Watch
    (Southridge High School,
    Miami, Fla.)
"Yes, I Can" Award, 78
YMCA, Seattle Metro Center,
    68, 69
Young American Medal for
    Bravery, 96, 116
Young Giraffe Award, 47, 150

Youth Crime Watch (Southridge
    High School, Miami, Fla.),
    34-39
Youth Speakers Speaking for the
    Truth, 47

# ABOUT THE AUTHOR

Barbara Lewis teaches fourth, fifth, and sixth graders in Salt Lake City, Utah. She has won over 30 awards and recognitions for excellence in teaching and writing and for her students' projects. Her students have initiated three laws in the Utah Legislature, instigated the amendment of a national law, brought about cleanup of a hazardous waste site, planted hundreds of trees, and obtained neighborhood sidewalk improvements. You can read about these children and others in Barbara's book, *The Kid's Guide to Social Action* (Free Spirit Publishing Inc., 1991).

Besides writing books, Barbara has written articles and short stories for many magazines. Her students' projects have also been featured in many national magazines and newspapers, in *The Congressional Record*, and on national and international television.

Barbara has lived in Indiana, New Jersey, Switzerland, and Belgium. She now resides in Utah with a charming husband, four "usually" charming children named Mike, Andrea, Christian, and Samuel, and an acrobatic goldfish that jumps out of the aquarium.

# Other Great Books from Free Spirit

### The Kid's Guide to Service Projects
Over 500 Ideas for Young People Who Want to Make a Difference
*by Barbara A. Lewis*
This guide has something for everyone who wants to make a difference, from simple projects to large-scale commitments. Kids can choose from topics including animals, the environment, hunger, politics and government, and more. For ages 10 & up.
*$10.95; 184 pp.; softcover; 6" x 9"*

### What Teens Need to Succeed
Proven, Practical Ways to Shape Your Own Future
*by Peter L. Benson, Ph.D., Judy Galbraith, M.A., and Pamela Espeland*
Based on a national survey, this book describes 40 developmental "assets" all teens need to succeed in life, then gives hundreds of suggestions teens can use to build assets wherever they are. For ages 11 & up.
*$14.95; 368 pp.; softcover; illus.; 7¼" x 9¼"*

### What Do You Stand For?
A Kid's Guide to Building Character
*by Barbara A. Lewis*
Young people need guidance from caring adults to build strong, positive character traits—but they can also build their own. This inspiring book invites them to explore and practice honesty, kindness, empathy, integrity, tolerance, patience, respect, and more. For ages 11 & up.
*$18.95; 284 pp.; softcover; B&W photos and illus.; 8½" x 11"*

### The Kid's Guide to Social Action
How to Solve the Social Problems You Choose—and Turn Creative Thinking into Positive Action
*Revised, Expanded, Updated Edition*
*by Barbara A. Lewis*
A comprehensive guide to making a difference in the world, this book teaches letter-writing, interviewing, fundraising, lobbying, getting media coverage, and more. For ages 10 & up.
*$16.95; 224 pp.; softcover; B&W photos and illus.; 8½" x 11"*

*To place an order or to request a free catalog of*
SELF–HELP FOR KIDS® *and* SELF–HELP FOR TEENS® *materials,*
*please write, call, email, or visit our Web site:*

**Free Spirit Publishing Inc.**
**400 First Avenue North • Suite 616 • Minneapolis, MN 55401-1724**
**toll-free 800.735.7323 • local 612.338.2068 • fax 612.337.5050**
**help4kids@freespirit.com • www.freespirit.com**